Harold Norse
The Love Poems
1940-1985

Also by Harold Norse

The Undersea Mountain
The Roman Sonnets of G.G. Belli
The Dancing Beasts
Olé
Karma Circuit
Selected Poems: Penguin Modern Poets 13
Hotel Nirvana
I See America Daily
Carnivorous Saint
Beat Hotel
Mysteries of Magritte

Copyright © 1986 by Harold Norse
Cover Photograph by Ronald Chase
Cover Design by Betsy Bayley
Typeset by Giles Bayley
Printed in the U.S.A. by McNaughton & Gunn of Ann Arbor, Michigan

Library of Congress Cataloging-in-Publication Data

Norse, Harold.
     Harold Norse, the love poems, 1940-85.

     1. Homosexuality, Male—Poetry. 2. Love poetry,
American. I. Title. II. Title: Love poems.
PS3527.O56H37 1986   811'.54   86-16785
ISBN 0-89594-204-6
ISBN 0-89594-203-8 (pbk.)

To the reader, with love

*The guns from the rooftops
are aimed at our hearts and genitals
with deadly accuracy*

*

*There's someone out there, I tell you,
who's the answer
to your prayers*

CONTENTS

Author's Foreword

III. CALIFORNIA (1968-1979)

V. CALIFORNIA (1980-1985)

VI. HOMO (1984-1985)

by Nina Glaser

FOREWORD

This collection of mostly homoerotic, but also heteroerotic, love poems spans four-and-a-half decades. It rose from the ashes of its predecessor, *Carnivorous Saint,* published in 1977, about which readers and reviewers continued to express a lively interest during the past decade. Born in the permissive '70s and now reborn in the oppressive '80s the carnivorous saint is still alive, if not always well, to remind us of the power of love and—let's not be hypocritical—lust. The principle of eroticism can never wholly die or we die with it. Anacreon, Archilochus, Catullus or Pindar, to name a few immortals, after thousands of years remind us of this.

And so Eros appears reborn here, in many forms and guises, strains and stresses, in more than seventy new poems and re-discovered early poems and in some revised from the earlier book. For various reasons I have discarded almost the same number, as well as the original graphics. The poems of the '80s clearly reflect the effects of two devastating plagues—the extreme Right heterosexist dictatorship and the equally horrendous presence of AIDS (two major setbacks for Gay liberation). *Saint* has metamorphosed to reassert the principle of Eros in a dangerously bigoted, fanatic moral climate. Without Eros who would or could exist?

Here is the personal record of erotic consciousness as it has existed for one writer in America, Europe and North Africa for almost five decades. I wish to thank John Gill of the Crossing Press for making this publication possible.

Harold Norse
San Francisco, 18 June 1986

I. NEW YORK (1940-1953)

Inside Out

Wearing myself inside out
like a coat put on in a rush
in public I seemed ridiculous
to the outside in.

It seems I revealed too much.
The lining of the self
and certainly the label
gave me away.

But in broad daylight
on Main Street I ran
among the crowds
and the traffic policeman

like a circus bear
with a gold ring in my nose.
I caused a great sensation
among the outside in.

New York, ca. 1940

YMCA Lounge

Behind the daily papers and cigarettes
they relax. Some read, most sit
and stare at *The Three Fates* on the wall
while Tschaikowsky's *Hamlet* overture
grieves. Eyelids droop. Talk rises, falls.

In the corridors boys leap
clutching small bags with the odor of keds.
Old men rasp to sailors stretching jersey thighs.
House phones ring at the desk. The Spanish motif
of hanging iron holders for flame-bulbs sheds
an embalming, funeral glow, reflects
the baldness of one with a turquoise ring
and pointed black shiny shoes. Odors

of hot athletes pervade the lounge, armpits
tangy with musk. The young men watch
each other with studied indifference, rise
and leave and return under stained glass
windows and porticoes. Eyes sometimes lock
and, with significant glances, the youths go
into the hall together murmuring
and ride the elevator to a room
or lavatory. The grieving overture
switches to *Gaité Parisienne*.

New York, ca. 1941

Tantalus

So many bodies have passed him by
virile limbs that tantalize
in scant clothes clinging
tight—it's a wonder he's not demented!

All day about the city
he padded the pavements, looking

Now he stands by the low wall
a wailing wall for his desires
which he conceals so carefully
you would not suspect them

He is mild, youngish, grave
and obsessed with passing
as anyone else

But his greatest obsession
sends him into the parks and streets
and will not let him sleep

New York, 1943

Stratagems

This simple painter of walls
during the noon hour
squatted before a laundromat
smoking and being
excessively smiled and talked at.

His hair, dusted with plaster, curled
on his forehead, blond sculpture.
The dust made up his lashes
whitely, thickened like a
detail of eyes on a Roman bust.

His lips were fresh and full
and red. The forearms
bulging slightly, tan
and powerful, bore strange tattoos.
He did not smile.

The smiler crouched
nervous beside him, spoke
swiftly, searching his face, darting
anxious glances at the
paint-smeared overalls, the arms,
the lips, the calm blue eyes,
then left.

Now I know his name, his taste, his touch
more intimately than the nervous boy
who could not act
and talked too much.

New York, 1.vii.53

II. EUROPE AND NORTH AFRICA (1954-1967)

Your Crooked Beauty. . .

Your crooked beauty, Hugo,
maims us. You are all
that hurts. Taking us
off guard with your virile
grace, good looks. But
you're crooked, you're bad news.
So you brought in the new
year that already had no good
in it for me, exiled
from a loveless country, took
what you wanted from its hiding place
among dirty clothing—30,000 liras—
then ground your teeth. I saw madness,
Hugo, death in your heroic
stony features, bones more enormous
than clubs, murderous jaws, the unseeing
statue stare of senselessness. Now
what's the use? At that price
your beauty is too expensive, leaving
neither regard for feelings
nor the rent.

Rome, New Year's Day, 1954

Roman Bar

Beside it the Forum
of Augustus

within
a steady flow
of life

lived in wicker
chairs

ranged round the
windows

letting
in the sun
&

views
of ancient ruins
At

tables young
men play
cards, joke

about each other's
rear ends, make
obscene gestures—they
drink

espresso, wink
suggestively—a
beggar strums a

guitar
the backroom is
for games—an old
dumpy grayhaired

grandma
dressed in
black takes out
pen &

ink—
laboring with tongue
& thumb she
writes a

letter
children peer
at candy

cigarettes are
sold

Rome, 1954

Island of Giglio

we sailed into the harbor
all the church bells rang
the main street on the crescent shore
hung iridescent silks from windows
stucco housefronts gleamed
rose, pistachio, peach
and a procession sang
behind a surpliced priest
carrying a burnished Christ
when I set foot on shore
a youth emerged from the crowd
barefoot and oliveskinned
and we climbed up rocky slopes
till dusk fell and close to the moon
at the mouth of a cave we made love
as the sea broke wild beneath the cliff

*

skeletons of fish, boats
on the beach, granite
boulders, juniper trees
and the town with winding
alleys; old men suck pipes
as the full moon leaps
like a flying fish &
shrinks up the sky; we
merge on the rocks
where waves run
up & down

Rome, 17.vi.54

Syracuse

The theatre of marble and moonlight has smooth steps like milk on stone. In the city the nymph is a green pool among papyrus and electric lights around her fountain. Half-nude boys squat on the rail, in the heat, cock in hand, inviting male tourists with smiles and nods. What else, prying at columns and fountains, can you ask but that the metope should live? It was here the fantastic wombshaped cave became a listening horn of licked lime, ear for tyrants; here the whisper of the condemned was borne upwards, past dripping walls, echoing lips of water, moans, midnight confessions, conspiracies. Outside, not so secure as a god, yet nearly, to the people monstrous, Dionysius, tyrant, at his ear of stone overheard the enormous cavern unsheathe its secrets.

Sicily, ca. 1954

Etruscan Fresco
(Tarquinia)

Was it against Nature when the bull
seeing the young men couple in the wood
pointed his huge horns and charged
the naked youths, bull's blood
storming his erect hot pizzle?
Three thousand years ago
the men who painted frescoes
to commemorate the dead
knew that lust was all that stood
between themselves and them.

Florence, 1954

On Translations of Catullus

Catullus, you'd bust your balls laughing!
For 2000 years they've fixed you like a horny cat—
the pedagogues can't take you straight.
Old pederast, they'll never make it
—not while they teach you how to write!

Rome, 1955

Catullus for Real
(Translations)

LV

The Search

Oramus, si forte non molestumst

If I may look for you without offense
I beg you, darling, where's your hiding place?
    I've searched each corner you frequent,
The lesser Campus and the Circus tents,
And in the Forum bookstalls where your face
Over some verses, by intelligence
Made more desirable, is usually bent.

But you were nowhere; from the hallowed white
Porphyry of Jove's temple, like a dog
    I ran, my tongue hung dry, a sight
For everyone to see. I stopped mid-flight
In Pompey's portico; the women gagged
With laughter when I quizzed them: "Spent the night
With me? Catullus, are you well? are you all right?"

But still I kept on asking for you: "Give me
My Camerius, you bitchy girls!"
    And one, baring her tits for me,
Says, "Look! He's hiding here, can't you see,
Between my hefty breasts!" Well, seeking pearls
In oysters is not harder, dear, than to be
Patient with you, nor the tasks of Hercules.

No, not if I were like that Cretan jailer
Brass-wrought, or bird-footed Perseus
    Or Ladas, or a heaven-scaler
Fording cloud-currents like that fleet sky-sailor
Pegasus, or the snowy team of Rhesus,
Could I catch up with you; add to my failure
The speed of gods and winds, my skill could not be frailer!

Though, Camerius, you yoked all these
Into my service, I should be worn out
    To the bone, fainting, on my knees

Hunting you down. O my sweet friend, please,
Do not deny yourself so proudly, flout
The love I bear. Don't mock my miseries;
Out with it, you can trust me—where are you apt to be?

Do the dove-white girls detain you? I'm above
Fits of jealousy, but if you keep
    Your tongue tied in your mouth, love
Between us will be wasted. Will you prove
You hate me? It pleases Venus—talk is cheap—
To hear our words. But if you're firm as Jove,
Let me, at least, possess a small share in your love.

Rome, 1954

XXXIII

O furum optime...

O slickest thieves at the public baths,
Vibennius and your fairy son!
The right hand of the father is predacious
and the son's behind remarkably voracious.
So beat it both of you, go to hell!
since everyone knows of the father's filching
and your ass, boy, is too hairy to sell.

Rome, 1955

C

Caelius Aufilenum...

Caelius for Aufilenus, Quintius for Aufilena—
    One boy is mad for the brother, and the other boy for the sister,
All of them the finest flower of Veronese youth.
    Here's the sweet brotherhood! Here it is!
The brotherhood of man! Which shall I vote for? Caelius, you:
    Your friendship was beautifully shown me—it was unique!—
When a mad flame scorched my genitals. Luck, then Caelius,
    May you be successful and potent in your love!

Rome, 1955

LXXXI

Nemone in tanto potuit populo esse, Iuventi...

Of all these people is there not one handsome man,
    Juventius, you might have chosen for yourself
Besides that friend of yours from the sickly area
    Of Pisaurum, paler than a whitewashed statue,
Who now is dear to you, whom you presume to prefer
    To me, your Catullus, not knowing what a rotten thing you're doing?

Rome, 1955

XV

Commendo tibi me ac meos amores

I am entrusting to you, Aurelius,
all I love most in the world, this boy, and beg
only a small favor. if you've ever valued
something beyond price, to be kept chaste and pure,
then guard this boy for me. I don't mean from strangers;
it is not the man in the street I fear; he's busy
about his own affairs. it's you,
you and your big prick
lusting after boys, molesting good and bad alike.
when you're outside you may waggle your erection
as much as you please at anyone you please. but spare this one,
it's not much to ask. but if lust
runs away with you, if your dirty mind runs amuck
and you betray me and my lover, you'll suffer,
I promise you, a terrible fate.
before the whole town's eyes, with your feet in chains,
I'll shove radishes and mullets up your ass.

San Francisco, Summer 1976

XVI

Pedicabo ego vos et irrumabo

I'll fuck and rim you both and suck your cocks
faggot Aurelius and fairy Furius
who believe I am immodest because of my verses
which, admittedly, are quite voluptuous.
but though the serious poet should himself be chaste
his poems are under no such strict necessity.

San Francisco, Summer 1976

XXI

Aureli, pater esuritionem

Aurelius, father of famine,
not this one only but of all hunger past
and future—you want to make love to my boy.
not even secretly: for you're always with him,
joking, sticking close to his side,
     trying every trick to tempt him.
       no good, it won't work.
while you're scheming against me,
I'll bugger you before you know it.
if you had a full belly I'd be quiet,
but as it is, what worries me is that
my darling will starve to death.
        so hands off
if you don't want me *to fuck you.*

San Francisco, Summer 1976

After Belli
(Translations)

LOT AT HOME

With their stout staffs in their left hand
Two pilgrims at the hour of *Ave Maria*
Were looking for the hotel in that area
Because one had a pain in his leg and couldn't stand.

There they met Mr. Lot, and he threw wide
The door, saying: "My house. Step inside."
And they answered him: "By gosh, tomorrow
You'll be the white-haired boy of this rotten borough."

Those were two angels, brother, whose tight britches
When the gay Gomorrhites saw them pass
Straightened all the dicks in the whole city.

And they arrived shrieking, those damn bitches,
"Lot, send down the pilgrims to us, so we
Can oblige each other by putting it up the ass!"

Rome, 1955

Ave Maria: after sundown; since all Biblical events took place in Belli's early 19th century Rome, as far as the speakers are concerned, time is reckoned by the Italian system, according to its Book of the Hours (translator's note).

Lot's Refreshment

So, already at Sodom and Gomorrah
Everyone was roasted and baked like mullet
And from so many families in that horror
The only one that escaped was that of Lot.

Without ever taking a breath or pulling the reins
The Patriarch kept running the whole day:
But then, as it usually is, to his daughters there came
With dusk a fantasy to want to lay.

But because on that far border they were sunk,
Not even one cock with a spark of life,
They said: "Daddy is sexy!" and they got him drunk.

Then having thrown two glances at his dumdumdangle
Those randy sisters happily all night
Divided between themselves the bang-bang-bang-o.

Rome, 1955

Dumdumdangle: in the original, *dumpennente,* a portmanteau word Belli created from *dum pendebat* from the *Stabat Mater* (translator's note).

Prick Poem

Well, call it the cock, dick, prick or peepee,
crank, dork, joint, pisser, sweetpea,

tootsie roll, lollipop, weenie, piece of meat,
sausage, salami, banana, somethin' to eat,

peter, boner, codpiece, flute or fife,
snake, cucumber, dingus, staff-of-life,

dong, prong, schlong, wang, hardon,
weapon, tool, piston, ramrod, gun,

shaft, stiff, bone, bishop, wick,
puddin', pope, pud, French tickler, joystick,

pipe, rod, knob, rolling pin,
John Thomas, stretch, grow-in-hand, stick-it-in,

what the old doc calls organ, member, phallus,
and his withered wife call penis, thing, priapus.

Rome, 1955/San Francisco, 1985

Ti Voglio Bene*

on the terrace
with cactus and geraniums
under the dome of Borromini
in the sun
wiping sweat
trickling
through thatch of bodyhair
I read and broil in   the olympic summer
as the date
gets buried
under a mess of days
and unmade beds
and nights
of sexy numeros
and I get stuck
in a vise of stone
of swirling angels
domes
fleshy frescoes
brown bodies
in Roman light
among marble fountains
saying *dove vai?*
and singing
ti voglio bene

Rome, 1956

* I love you

Victor Emmanuel Monument (Rome)

The marble typewriter or "wedding cake"
is large enough to shelter in its side
several armies; as it is, they keep
a squad of *bersaglieri* there, the hand-
picked of all Italy, the flower to guard

this monsterpiece. In scarlet fez and blue
pompom halfway down the back, like birds
of paradise they strut, their bodies hard
and flashing flesh by sunlight or moonlight
with all the brilliance of the male panache.
And this is all they have to do. What else
on seventeen cents a day, in Italy?
Any night by the white marble ploy
discovers them in whispered assignations
picking up extra cash, from man and boy.

Rome, ca. 1956

Massaccio

I think of you, Massaccio
    in the city
  of feudal gloom

apprenticed
to Ghiberti
      laboring on those dazzling doors
    that swung to paradise

hungry helper, hard up youth
you held the birth of man
in your hands

then, on your own, you worked
on the tabula rasa of a thousand years
    (blank wall of the church)
with figure, form, shade and light

you worked with Christ
your brother, like you
with no place to lay his head

color flowed as never before
form fit content as never before

still broke, anonymous
you gave to those worse off than you
and went to your death
    in Catholic Rome
starved in that Heaven of Christ-on-earth
    at twenty-seven

Florence, 1956

The Singing Gallery

On a cracked wall in Italy
I saw something the bomb passed by
in a dark church aisle:
Piero della Francesca
set his seal of light
in colors that speak yet.
And Luca della Robbia
made thick marble sing
his joyous song
of Renaissance boys.
They sing to me.

Now it's rockets to the moon,
we change sex like underwear,
we believe in science.
All right, men must have myths.
I'll take The Singing Gallery.

Florence, 1956

The Secret Pornographic Collection

In the National Museum of Naples
on this hot afternoon
lamps, braziers, jugs, caskets,
kitchenware—ancient food
from the buried city of Pompeii,
fixed in cold lava, a world
of naked pleasure: tripods

holding basins or braziers—one
mounted on marble, goat-legs forming
three ithyphallic young Pans
with tilted erections, raised hands
while dark young men
browse languidly and stroke
themselves
joking, touching their past
as they touch their sex
in sensual recognition
as if the church
and two millennnia
had never happened

Naples, 1958

La Raccolta Pornographica is the secret pornographic collection of the
Museum, so-called because it houses the erotica of ancient Pompeii and
Herculaneum, from which the bronze tripod was liberated, by Alexandre
Dumas *père*, I believe, who became curator under Garibaldi in 1860, and to
whom we probably owe its open display in one of the galleries, although I
cannot vouch for the accuracy of my scholarship since changes of moral climate
have constantly affected this collection's accessibility. During the Fascist era,
for example, it was made off limits to the public.

Piccolo Paradiso

For Giorgio

let the age hang itself! we've had
four marvelous days together
    no news reports   only music
      & no serious discussions

plenty of wine   the best
from the islands
    white
      falerno & ischian
      & lacrima cristi
          we've made up
        for months
      of loneliness
        hard work
      nastiness
          of 'superiors'

we may not live
very well or long
our mistakes are perhaps too great
to bear correction
at this midpoint
of our lives (you're somewhat younger)
surely too great
to make up for the lengths we go to
hide them
è cosi. . .that's
how it goes
but at least
we're ahead of the game
we've stolen a march
on the dead   the herd
if the return to grayness
sharp tempered weapons
of those who force life
into corners
is more than we can bear
remember this
the wine
the ladder
of stars
climbing vesuvius
outside my window
the waves
banging into
smooth tufa caves
& the opera
as we lay together
remember

Naples, 1958

Classic Frieze in a Garage

i was walking thru the city past umber embassies
& pine-lined palaces
fat palms beside balconies
the heat something
you could really touch

                    the kids with cunning
                          faces
               after americano sailors

               —thinking of nerval *rends-moi le pausilippe*
                  et la mer d'Italie & living
                        on the hill   posillipo   under
               a gangster's dancefloor
                                        among goldfinches

                          on the bay of naples
                           in a stone cottage
                        over tufa caves in which the sea
                          crashed in winter   sweet gerard
                          one hundred years
                    have made the desolation greater

               the tower is really down & the sun blackened
                     beyond despair   the loudspeaker drowns
                        finches   cliffs   caves
                     all in the hands of racketeers
               yet i have passed by time dreaming thru this
                        fantastic wreck

               walking thru incendiary alleys of crowded laundry
                     with yellow gourds in windows &
                     crumbling masonry of wars
                           human corruption
                     so thick & hopeless that i laugh

               when suddenly i saw among the oil & greasy rags
                     & wheels & axles of a garage
                     the carved nude figures of
                           a classic frieze
                     there above the dismantled
                     parts of cars!

          perfect! garage
               swallows sarcophagus!
          mechanic calmly spraying
                 paint on a
                       fender
          observed in turn by lapith & centaur!

                          —33—

                                    flow
                    of unthinking flesh!
                              frank thighs! eyes
                    of aphrodite!

              the myth of the mediterranean
                    was in that garage
                  where the brown wiry
              youths saw nothing unusual
                    at their work
                  among dead heroes & gods

              but i saw hermes in the rainbow
                    of the dark oil on the floor
                          reflected there
                    & the wild hair of the sybil
                        as her words bubbled
              mad & drowned
                              beneath the motor's roar

                                    Naples, 1958

I am in the Hub
of the Fiery Force

red for fire red for lava red for blood
  red for the savage meridional sun
    for the walls of herculaneum
      the mouths of nymphomaniacs
        the gums of satyrs their monstrous pizzles
          their dreams their bestial dreams
            for the villas at the volcano's foot
              the scorpion's sting the dying screams

red for hibiscus rose amaryllis
  red for phallus red for yoni
    red for pompeii red for stabiae
      for the naked men fucking in frescoes
        the cymbals of shrieking priests of cybele
          their orgies eunuch rites of castration
            for drums and pipes of loaded bacchus
              for snaky jagged tongues of fury

—34—

red for pain for raw for wild for bull
for wine for lion for kill for hell
for suck for lust for whip for drug
for high for bust for crime for thirst
obsessed with red as the universe burns
i am in the hub of the fiery force
the red heat of the conflagration
o cosmos turn! turn! thy flaming wheel!

Naples, 1958

Green Ballet

For W. I. Scobie

overhead
on the bridge
trucks are speeding under angels

parks are empty & leaves are falling

erect in mud
their shoes slurping
on the riverbank two people
are breaking laws with their hips

at the top of the steps a sign reads

WORKERS ONLY   NO TRESPASSING

one is in rags
he is 16
he has red lips

the other is a man
who sees god as he looks up
at the boy who looks down

the boy is thinking of the whore with the man
he spied on in the shadows
by Hadrian's Tomb
as he clutches the man's ears

        tensing his thick
thighs
        & they come

the man thinks *god god*
        & the terror!
any moment all's reversed
only the world's uniform **THUD**

all this time the Tiber sucking
        sucking
the fat mud

                                        Rome, 1960

In Italian the title, *balletti verdi,* means gay scenes or scandals, in the
vernacular.

The Pine Cone

        the insane police
          dog yelping
        for a pine cone
        to retrieve from the
                waves
          his reflex joy
                mad anguish
        when it is not thrown
                WOOF!

          he rolls
        over the cone
                tearing
        at sand
          with forepaws

        as Spanish fishermen
          watch and
                laugh

          I chase the flesh
        as that dog chases
                the pine cone

o Christ!
the earth
   and sea never
looked so new
   so perishable

   I walk
up streetstairs
Carrer del Gats in
      Benidorm where
        highstepping ringdoves
spread fantails
   in cotes like César
Girón approaching
  a bull
  ass and head stuck out
   arms like
banderillas
   my god what swagger!

I stand looking at the
  Spanish night
of shimmering suns and
       galaxies

my blood
  throbs in black gulfs
   a car hoots
down the road

Benidorm, 1956

Gothic Quarter, Barcelona

A shopkeeper kicks in the head
of an old beggar, a thief holds a knife
to a tourist's throat, a woman screams
raped by a drunk in a doorway
of marble and puke, young macho studs
attack 2 drag queens in full view
of cheering crowds shouting *Olé*
as a birdlike woman on a barstool
with unblinking eyes and flourwhite face

like a mime or a clown
stares
straight
ahead
immobile for hours
and a hunchback begs and insults the crowd
while sailors from the Sixth Fleet wander
drunk and horny under Moorish balustrades
and rotting stone columns
where Arabs in burnooses check out
bleached whores under stained glass windows
while gipsies howl flamenco
under festooned city lights
forming graceful loops overhead
and a dog farts
and a cripple waves his stump
and a landlord with a dead rat face
cruises a sailor who rubs his crotch
with the look of a striptease artist
and under the portico the whores
stand on duty
a whore who walks like a truckdriver
a whore who writes poetry
a whore who looks like a drag queen
and a drag queen who looks like a whore
and there's a macho stud
who turns gay when he's drunk
and burns cigarette holes in his hand
because he hates what he is
although everybody loves him
and the students sing and drink wine all night
under the lamps of Gaudi in the Plaza Real
the crucible of Spain
where the whole country ferments like wine
like cheese like painting like music
like birth
or death
or dreams
or war
or love

Barcelona, November 1978

The Barcelona Girls and Boys

They look familiar
out of the Thirties
where I left them
back in
Brooklyn
long ago

But this is Barcelona
after 40 years
of the Generalissimo
to keep them on ice
to stop the clock
and the heart

Now Spain's a democracy
and these young women
are madly in love
with social ideas
and with their young men
who wear leather jackets
and rough beards
and carry books
for the revolution

They touch one another
in streets, cafés and restaurants
with much tenderness

But I would ask of them
only this:
make your revolution
for the freedom to love
either sex
in any way
as need demands

Do not become the pigs of the future.

Barcelona, 6.xi.78

France

now France   yesterday Italy   & it's fall
special Paris light   slant on treetops   gray
buildingtops   clear   hard   like French eyes
bulge of intellect   chalcedony eyes
& architecture creates   the sky

     will someone stop me in the street   saying
     how wonderful!   we don't know each other?!
        just walk arm in arm
          & never ask our names!
make love at sight!   anonymous as monks!
         esperanto lips!
     Africa in my arms!   Near East!

but how to slow down   I'm running away
     are those my arteries   or steel tracks?
        stations in the dawn   old man
sourly pushing letters   in huge sacks
        are they my unfinished plans?

        Paris of leaves   beards   duffel coats!
am I interested in radio telescopes?
        the kind that look inside the moon?
     parabolic mirrors?   limits of the solar system?
Izvestia follows me around   sneers at my life
        no wonder I'm feeling blue

I'm here to tell you of a finer fate
     to explore trees
        listen to colors
          pick the golden flower
            feel under someone's duffel coat
              for the clear light
              of the void

down on your knees!   pray to the holy human body!
     worship god in the fork of the thighs!
        I can't blow the 'socialist victory'
     nor raise any flag but my lilywhite ass
to all the silly nations who want me to choose sides

I've chosen   orgasm/feeling/smell/soul
freedom of dream   who is freer than when he dreams?

I choose the light of the sky   over the boulevards
   & the bookstalls   full of sexy pictures
    & occult prophecies   THE EARTH

Paris, 1960

Chez Popoff

melo chez popoff
melo at the monaco
melo in storyville
melo eating pink loukoum
melo with one gold tooth
piscean melo digs the hidden poetry of death
turns on in my room with words of crucifixion
betrayed by pinball machines
telling tales of three-day hard ons
having it rubbed with hot cantari in french guiana
he offers himself for coins
he gooses tourists on the boul' mich
his chocolate chest startles the quays
the quay of pont neuf & le petit pont
sheathed in mirrors & lies
his look is telepathic
his kisses are black lightning
he paints dark blobs of pain
in his room dark with death
in his room light with laughs
in his eyes dark with light
o unreachable bird of smoke
black swan of sad jazz landscapes

Paris, ca. 1961

Place de Furstemburg

the sweet young thing
passes around the hat
and the French cat sings
AH AH AH lalalala
with his guitar
and the derrières of St. Germain
are pink and blue buds
in the sun and everyone
is drinking beer
and eating cacahuètes
in a mimic movie of lips and tits
while bombs shatter windows
next to the cafés
and flies buzz in the sugar
and wine glasses
and I leave
for a calm little square
with 4 plane trees
and a street lamp
Place de Furstemburg
where flat on his belly
a lotus boy
with radiant tan
and dirty feet
dozes beside a thick green
cardboard folder
from the Beaux Arts Academy
as the concierge at the window
her leathery arms
folded on the sill
sits very gray
very sad
very old
one hand against her mouth
looking out at him
and suddenly he looks up
from the bench
drowsily
and I stare
as if perhaps at a painting
by Delacroix
whose studio is closed for repairs

in this same square
and next day I am back
for the boy the birds the concierge
but nothing remains
not even the trees
just 4 gaping holes
where they had been

Paris, June 1961

From the 6th Arrondisement

(Paris journal, September 1961)

Paris, you have ceased
to be the *cité*
plein de rêves. But you
are still the satyr-city, kissing
couples in the streets, young
bodies & fantastic
styles of dress—
the *youngest* city in Europe!
half your Frenchmen just kids.
I'm envious, have a
toothache & a hard-on
and feel sorry for myself
in Paris in the Spring.

*

9, Rue Gît-le-Coeur (the Beat Hotel)

armpit odor of bearded boys—guitar
riffs, bongo drums, voices & candlelight
up at Milt Mezzrow's, Room 30—swinging
real nice...but at 10 p.m. the concierge
warns: "the cops are coming if you don't stop!"
"Yeah, man, like if you're happy, the fuzz
comes. If you're living, the heat shows.
Man, let's get to the Andes...gotta face
reality...the bomb is here & there ain't
no room for us both."

*

He goes from hurt to hurt.
"The thick veil of Maya
that must have covered my heart
is not so easily removed."
His devotion is impressive.
He wants to be "self-realized"
yet seeks out suffering
& cruelty in his men.
We hit bottom, touch
silence.
Poor F. will you ever
know what you feel?

*

Chlorophyll & blood...and the sky
with bars at the end. Paris, old whore....
I limit my life. Fatigue.
All them germs!
Police! Eye contact
is dangerous. But couples still kiss,
walk with linked hands—clutch
each other. I'm
the odd one, a small time Genet, haunting
pissotières (like Gide) and even those
have been torn up by de Gaulle.

*

Masturbate wildly. 3 a.m. A knock.
Throw open the door, naked.
Arab I used to know. No place
to stay. Crash here? OK. Shows
me his boat ticket. "I return
to Tunis in a week." Removes
shoes & socks, revealing huge
dirty feet, swollen from tramping. Asks
for scissors, slowly cuts
all his fingernails, then toenails.
Removes gray houndstooth suit.
Climbs into bed, mutters, "Je suis
très fatigué." Loud snores.
Next morning, without a word, he dresses

& laying a cold hand briefly on my arm leaves.
Masturbate wildly.

*

Rue Bonaparte. 8 p.m. Paratroops
in scarlet berets at pinball "flippers"
with whores of both sexes. Smoke & coffee.
A paratroop winks at me, his whore frowns.
Around midnight, police wagon pulls up.
Out jump the keystone cops, tommyguns ready.
About to go thru the usual spot check when
there's a shot from the rue St. Benoît, around
the corner (probably a paper bag). The fuzz
turn white, awkwardly tug at pistol holsters
(very strange because their tommy guns are ready)
and disappear on the run, Mack Sennett style,
tilting at all angles. We laugh and pay,
whores, paratroops, hustlers, pimps & crooks,
& move on, in leisurely fashion.

*

Fishboy

Fishboy knocks. He is 18
with powerful smooth thighs.
Stands holding a cigarette
between two flippers,
honey hair sleek as a seal's.
Unforgettable aroma, musk
of something wild as wet seaweed. But
he's just French farmboy hustling
in Paris. Asks for a 'loan'
of 5 francs. I nod and help him
drop his pants, like peeling
a layer of skin. He bends
to plant sweet lips on mine, grinding
his hips as we pant and grunt.

Later I light 2 Gauloises,
give him 5 francs
and off he floats.

*

French Country Boys....

French country boys have rigged themselves a simple primitive contraption, a fuck machine to bugger themselves, says my friend Van B., who ought to know as he is a rich American of French descent who owns a castle in the country, where he has spent some 50 pederastic summers. Fishboy, when I ask about this, calmly agrees.

The thought forms: to bugger Fishboy is the answer to all men's most cherished fantasies (in Morocco they would kill for him), for not only has he the most extraordinary buns I have ever seen (and I am an aficionado), white, smooth, flaring, voluptuous, perfectly calipered by a Blakean God—but his thighs must be the world's most desirable.

(Yet he wanders around Paris with his clean tight pants, peddling that gorgeous ass for a few lousy francs—thank God!—and many nameless assholes are put off because of this anomaly.)

Many years later in San Francisco I came across Margaret Mead's statement to the Washington Press Club: "I think rigid heterosexuality is a perversion of nature."

The newspapers did not report the reaction of her audience; but any man gazing at Fishboy's naturally flushed hairless cheeks and crimson lips, not to speak of those nether cheeks, must surely feel the same or be a pervert.

Think of the tremendous *unnatural* effort at suppression of homosexual urges, largely unconscious (the common state of the world), that most men make all their lives (except gay ones, who are really the most heroic because they do what others merely dream of doing.)

I regret to report that Fishboy disappeared from circulation before I got around to fulfilling my desire. A moral of some sort must surely be implicit here (strike when the buns are hot?)....

Paris, ca. 1961

A Gay Night

I drove them out last night
to a gay club where faggots dance
16 kms. from Paris.
we found a few desolate queens
seated at tables in a large room
with copper pots on the walls, a loudspeaker
played sentimental tunes from the Thirties.
this old dyke in a tweed suit
runs the joint. we order beer.
things picked up after awhile.
soon everybody was dancing
like 'normal couples'. two bald queens
clasped each other round the waist,
the short one in a white turtleneck,
his ass stuck out, danced
spine arched, head coyly tossing
from side to side. the place
became a barnyard: shrieking freaks,
cackling falsettos to Viennese waltzes,
plucked eyebrows over thin moustaches,
goosing and horsing and oinking.
have you ever seen a freakshow dancing?
André danced with everybody
while Mustapha sat and smoked my Gauloises Bleues.
they were drumming up trade.
"See that grayhaired old one?" a sheep
with glasses, a few tables away,
looked over and grinned. later,
they disappeared in an Aronde.
I drove back with André, who never shut up for a moment
about the lousy bunch of cheap fairies.
at the Mabillon around 1 a.m. Mustapha showed.
"What happened?" I asked. "Nothing." he spat
in disgust. "You made nothing?" "Nothing,
I tell you! He wouldn't pay. He owns 2 cars,
the Aronde and a Studebaker,
and he wouldn't pay. Merde!"
he smacked his fist into his palm.
"Well, that's what I told le petit André," I said.
but it served him right.
he never said thanks for a free lunch,
free beer, nylon shirt, broke dates,

stood everyone up, basking
in the aura of his looks.
as for his pintsized pal, André,
with the big droopy Arab nose,
he has the nerve to charge
100 francs. Demented bitch!

Paris, 1961

The Death of 9 Rue Gît-le-Coeur

For William S. Burroughs

a bat flies in thru the window at 3 in the afternoon
slides under the table and disappears...postcard from chinatown san fran
suddenly drops from the ceiling out of nowhere
everything is normal, nothing is strange
black bat flits slow motion to the table's bottom
where it vanishes

everything is permitted...nothing is true

indo-chinese lady in silk parts bamboo curtains & glides downstairs
giant spade from french guiana slips thru mirrors turned on
dreamachine spins shapes & colors round & round
opening up visions as it crashes the sight barrier & alters the brain
a great american writer receives whole episodes in his sleep
for the novel of new consciousness

> prophetic utterances
> nameless assholes
> agonized angels
> end of poetry
> huge genitals
> buttfucked boys

sad movies on the sea wall
drowned islands float up from adolescent place forgotten
drifting croon of shrunken ether heads
iridescent bubbles of shifted consciousness

it is over   ...finished...a dream
workmen hammer & plaster in halls full of tools & cement
old spiral staircase white with wind
no more army surplus parkas
no more guitars
no more horns
the old café FERMÉ POUR TRAVAUX
ghostly espresso machine gapes on dusty shelves
    chairs gape
nobody now where we used to gather & talk
"very uncool to carry a piece"

mirrors of 1910 kept nagging me
flashing nails in your cheating naked brain
kept seeing America dying in swamp green smiles
a bat flies out of your eyes
dreamachine turns on the boy's agonized cells
the room flushed out by your mouldy expeditions
took possession of his falling flesh

"Beat Hotel," Paris, 1963

A threnody for the hotel in Paris internationally known as the "Beat Hotel"
where H.N. lived with William Burroughs, Brion Gysin, Gregory Corso, et al.,
and where the Cut-up method was born and *Naked Lunch* assembled for
publication. Everyone decamped, so to speak, in 1963 when the motherly old
woman who owned the place, Mme. Rachou, sold it to retire to an apartment
across the street, and some years later died. In her youth she was a waitress in
a restaurant frequented by Monet, Pissarro, Picasso, etc. At the hotel she ruled
with an iron hand, a legend in her own right.

Vence

Matisse and Chagall painted church walls
and D. H. Lawrence died here
lightning rips the hills of the Côte d'Azur
quake destroys Skoplje in Yugoslavia
and prophecies work through vast illusion and dream
a firefly glows on my bedsheet a star in my bed
and I bomb a giant spider spray him with Flytox
fearing the wary dance of his spiderhood

I watch him crawl and shrivel on the shower floor
thinking Will I meet death by Heavenly Flytox
lightning bolt or shift of the earth crushed
in agonized death throes caught in insect pursuits?
here in this country house no mescaline jewels nor laughing gas
hashish or kif can turn me on come crackup of this world
I kiss the Sweet Young Thing at my cottage door (he is sixteen today)
where we stand speechless and gazing in the summer night

Vence, 1963

Cannes

Near the Croisette the jeunesse dorée
glitter in nylon briefs.
They cruise among deck chairs,
lotions and parasols,
taking in suntans
with swift expert appraisal.
To watch them, you'd think
they had lost something in the sand.
They glance quickly
at sprayed hair and coppery thighs
with an air of boredom, shifting
their attention as if waiting
for someone who doesn't show.
Like yachts they twitch and strain
at anchor. A well-contrived
apocalypse would hardly disturb
the routine. In the evening
dressed with casual care
they fish around café tables
checking out seafood, styles, breasts
and muscles with equal zeal.
Whatever they talk about it's flesh
they're stalking with such élan, though
hinted at in slick repartee. It looks
like a fun game on this hot
Riviera—but the casualties

are high. In bars and hotels
when the fleet's in, the atmosphere's
international and gay. When
the gobs leave, there's a kind
of business-as-usual ennui
in town. Picasso had a villa
here. I recall mainly the heat,
cream-puff façades, chic languor.
And a gendarme who wouldn't believe
my passport and almost booked me
for strolling on the Croisette one night
impersonating an American.
I only half-convinced him parleying
French with a New York post-nasal drip.
When he left, grumbling, I muttered: Céline.
The 6th fleet lay in offshore darkness: chill air
warned of summer's end. A few girls,
drunk, flapped like beached fish, gasping
as they kissed their garçons. Cannes,
elegant and impersonal—a casino
of the would-be heart, spinning
a roulette wheel, like the sea
that rolls endless waves of chance toward lovers.
But not, to be sure, in a passionate way.

Cannes, 1963

Djema'a El Fna, Marrakech

Ragged listeners smoke and are carried away on magic carpets
A storyteller squats in the center of a crowd of beggars
Narrating A Thousand And One Nights as I sip mint tea
Snakes squirm at my feet naked boys covered with flies sleep on the
ground
Aladdin lamps glint in the carbide glow desert music everywhere
At magic stalls with evil eyes bones and monkey hair
Atmosphere thick with hashish kif and fantasy
And I'm swept up in the pipe dream of Arabia

Marrakech, 1962

Six for Mohammed Rifi:

To Mohammed at the Café Central

Tangier
sun and wind
strike the medina mosque

Mohammed
seventeen years old
puffs his kif pipe
sipping green mint tea
where blue phallic arches
rise among white walls
and berber rugs

the muezzin traces ALLAH
thru the moon's
loudspeaker
over casbah roofs
of Socco Chico

moneylenders
also sip mint tea
but Mohammed's eye
brilliant and black
darts among gray tourists
for a simpático friend
and glances at transistors
covetously
and tattooed mammas
you-youing
papoosed in laundrybags
peeping thru djellabas

the crescent sun plucks rugs
on lightning terraces
and dries
ten thousand years
in a second!

Tangier/Paris, 1962

To Mohammed on Our Journeys

I was the tourist
el simpático
and your brother offered you
and also himself

I forgot about your brother
and we took a flat in the Marshan
with reed mats and one water tap
about a foot from the floor
and we smoked hasheesh
and ate well and loved well
and left for the south
Essaouira, Fez, Marrakech
and got to Taroudant
thru the mountains
and bought alabaster kif bowls
for a few dirhams and watched
the dancing boys in desert cafés
kissing old Arabs and sitting on their
laps, dancing with kohl eyes, and
heard the music down in Joujouka
in the hills under the stars
the ancient ceremony, Pan pipes
fierce in white moonlight
and the white walls with hooded figures
stoned on kif for eight nights
and the goatboy in a floppy hat
scared us, beating the air
with a stick, beating whoever came close,
Father of Skins, goat god,
and the flutes maddened us
and we slept together in huts

San Francisco, 7.xi.72

To Mohammed in the Hotel of the Palms

behind the glass wall

                          i see blue limbs
                          black fungus noses

        thighs knee caps
                "i have the taste of the infinite"

ylem
       primoridal squinch   the universe crushed into
                                        a seed
nothing will satisfy me
                     i write green ballets & hollow journeys
caught in the etheric web of yr crotch
                   a hairy ocean of darkness

                          doors of pearl
                 open to fiery radiance
majoun madness
          down marrakech alleys
   the   djemaa el fna
squirming   with snakes
     in carbide glow

black gnaoua dancers!   lash sword!   flash teeth!
  under the barrow
    broiling in sleep   mouth
& nostrils buzzing with flies
                    genitals thick swollen
out of big tear in pants
               derelict 14 yr old street arab
      cameras   snapping
    like teeth

and who
        are you little arab
           i shared my visions
                  and ate
        black hasheesh candy with
the doors of yr body   flung open
        we twitched in spasms
         muscular convulsions
           heavenly epilepsy on the bed
     in the hotel of the palms
    prolonged orgasm
    uncontrollable joy
           of leaving the mind

Athens, 1965

To Mohammed at the Height

the moment widens—your voice
VAST across the room—my
head explodes into con
scious speed an ache
shoots along the
nerve of my left eye pushing to
the center above my nose—
your browngold skin
dance flute laugh
yes
everything lives
because I love you
ALL
levels
at once
brain flickers
nosebridge pinches
bright cells full of happening
this can not
END

Tangier/Paris, 1962

To Mohammed at Parting

the wind hurls through the straits
white ruffs on greenblue
water I will cross
to Spain

your bag is packed for the bus
to Melilla
back to the Rif

I see your mountain hut
the scrawny sheep
rugged Berber tribesmen
scrape in the fields
you will scrape

bye bye Mouniria
so long kid

Tangier/Paris, 1962

To Mohammed at the End

the boat
slid from the
dock into
nothing
i
watched
the sprayed
wake
churn green
silk water
peaks till
mist
twisted the
white town—a
face
followed
flashing sand
& wind & cheap
hotels—a face
will follow
voices
cities
& after
a year
or two i'll
grab a boat
on a water
chain
pulling
me back
to turn me
on
again

Tangier/Torremolinos/Athens, 1962/63

Carnivorous Saint

we dig up ancient shards
clicking cameras
among the dying cypresses
choked by Athenian smog.

yet cats continue basking
in the hazy sun
the chained goat sways in ecstasy
the Parthenon looks down from creamy heights
lichen and rust nibble the pediments
and tourist feet break the spell
of antiquity's vibrations.

the grass hits
as I look at rusty orangeade caps
thinking Who needs nuclear Apollo?
thermonuclear Minerva?
Nike crashing to grand finale?

we need the anti-Christ
who is probably playing football around the corner
the sweet boy who used to be called Eros
and wants us to be happy.

bring back the carnivorous saint
whose mother is no virgin
she's Our Lady of Peace Movements
to ban the bomb and clean up the air
she'll wave her umbrella and change the world.

ah yes, when the grass hits
old worlds burn down and new worlds form
in clouds of brown monoxide morning.

Athens, Jan. 1964

Under the Night Sky

Helen applies nivea oil to my crevices
you're beautiful she says
you have that lived-in look
and I like the white adobe hut
where we are at home
on the beach with the old gold mill
abandoned out front
near the "aztec" ruins
of Skyros
morning glory on the vine
two little fishes in,a pitcher
muscat grapes ripening
sandlilies outside the door
of the cottage
that we leave tomorrow
I pluck some basil leaves
and gobble grapes
and think of the night sky
under which we sit
smoking too much
whispering together
of hurting
and being hurt
can love after so many
errors, after so much
pain and fear exist?
under the night sky
on the Aegean shore
on the edge of a precipice
we kiss

Skyros, 1964

Giant Cruiser

Giant cruiser with yellow funnel
and blue sign: RODOS
(Rhodes) glittering among white houses
like sugar cubes, white sailors
and white birds

while at café tables
tongues wag languidly
like the tide

sensuality nags the nerves
around the port
where sunbrown boys
with hairy legs and bellies
and creamy blond girls down from the north
sniff the air voluptuously
on an eternal cruise

then from the Naval Academy
on the wharf a bugle blares
everyone stands at attention
in various stages of uninterest
a boat horn breaks
the military ritual
and the pleasure boat—SARONIS—
floats into the harbor
as barelegged bathers float
into restaurants, cafés
and other lives

Hydra, 1965

Conversation Galante

"Mind if I sit down?"
  "Okay. Have a cigarette."
"I could write a novel about my suffering.
    The whole town knows about me.
That boy has made me lose my self-respect."
"What else is new?"
        "Maybe I'll cut my throat."
            "What time?"
    "He won't let me suck him off anymore!"
"Humiliating."
            "What am I gonna do?"
                        "Well, wrap
a 5-pound-note around it—most powerful
    aphrodisiac in Greece!"

"You too!
You're making fun of me. Oh god,
I love him!"
                              "The donkey boy
          has twelve inches—"
          "Maybe I'll dance with him tonight."
"With who?"
                    "The donkey boy—make Yanni jealous!"
          "Mark, you're a fool."
                    "Thanks. I'm gonna get drunk
          on ouzo and dance to the juke all night."
"Oh, you silly Dutch queen!
          I'm gonna call you Wilhelmina."

Hydra, 1965

White Terraces

To Princess Zinaide Rachevsky, in memoriam

1

Beautiful ruthless, dangerous, spendthrift, generous, selfish, violent,
the princess tried everything from striptease queen, movie starlet, royal
marriage, poetry and painting, to becoming a Zen monk with a shaven
head in Nepal, where she died mysteriously, thus ending her search for
impossible enlightenment, just as she was beginning to resemble Mme.
Blavatsky in her forties, her spiritual double (but not her physical one
for Zina was slender), half-charlatan, half-magician. Zina had been
busted for dope and prostitution, among other things, cut off from
three vast fortunes for her crimes, but in the end was a real artist, that
is to say talented and treacherous. I do her homage as an unforgettable
bitch with class and charisma. She held court on the island of Hydra
and in Athens, where I last saw her.

2

guitars on white terraces
with cicadas and typewriters
and near-naked girls
and heavy stoned fucking in moonlight

and the island, they said, was magical
full of evil vibrations
(dogs were killed for sport)
an American scholar's Mom got raped
by the donkey boy
with the hugest dick in the port
secretly had by the scholar

who didn't know whom to be jealous of
and wrote a bad poem about it
and fell into the harbor
among the other jellyfish
and got fished out
moaning, "I wanna die!"

some did Greek dances with the fishermen
until they collapsed under the moon
brains rotten with retsina
passed out against whitewashed walls

some got busted for pot and spent 5 years in Tartaros
writing *Notes from Underground*
raped in their imaginations by Greek convicts

some became pop singers
some crouched with fear on street-stairs
their minds crumbled with breakdown
and the I Ching could not save them

some took acid and "saw the Light"
and went off to lick postage stamps in India
learning humility at the feet of gurus
giving up all possessions

some took poison and some blew out their brains
and Zen could not save them
nor Wu Wei
nor their name in a book
and their astrological chart was lousy

Hydra, 1965

A Big Fish

For Kostas Tachtsis

    300 pounds of blubber
flat on her back in Piraeus
jellyrolls and squirms, shakes her tits
    120 pounds of Yankee sailor
blond babyface puts it in
    2 poets masturbate on him

    the fat greek whore
got sentimental, heaving hugging moaning
as he made us do it everywhichway!

    Renna the Great White Whale!
little Davy flounders as he sticks it in
leviathan—his big harpoon—we
    stick it to *him!*

he shoves it to his orchids and we flower in one glooey
freakish ecstasy of momentary meat! everybody
    kissing and hugging—it was great!

Renna
    whose life savings went
one night—her loverpimp left her
beached—gaping swollen mammal in the street—
big fish for the fleet!

Athens, ca 1965

Karma Circuit

pale boy of the north with the dark spanish eyes
and hebrew mind who crossed my path thru poetry i ching
talking of superconscious telepathic coincidental changes
of the eternal now

hitching thru paradoxical zen
circuits of enlightenment
malmo—hydra
helsinki—ibiza
speaking the passwords karma oracle paranoia hexagram connections

finland is white and you had need of moving into blue
of summer's southern gold to find the way
to cross the bridge

what bridge? the bridge you always come to where
you stop and turning back must ask the question where

and everyone you meet is really you—another you
on wavelengths without separation
no frontier between selves or lands—all you's and me's

we sit up half a night the lamp burns low the kittens race
in the garden scratch at the cottage door as donkeys sob
their animal heats beneath the window
in the rubbish dumps outside

you screamed your poems in rotterdam tore down the german flags
hoisted the flag of israel breathing flames of kerosene
and you were busted for it

wild as your lapland flute
    kissed by birds and fish
        with swinging dragon fire
            traveling to the point/no point

            you leave all words and thoughts
          for sound beyond sound
        silence beyond speech

i'm oxidized by your mouth

Hydra, 1965

Addio

For Julia Chanler-Laurin

i have sat on the oldest throne in europe
            & heard the peacock scream in the ruins
i have drunk from the castalian fountain
            that the latin poets called
                the source of inspiration

& patted the umbilicus of the world in delphi

i have seen the sun
    on red columns
        & gold columns
            & blue monkeys
& seen the king of the lilies
  emerge
      from the flaming wall
         of crete
      feathered initiate
         staring tall & young
           from the earthquakes of time

& at the oracle of apollo
    heard the pythoness
        from the rock   :   CHOOSE

i knelt among the hollyhocks in the olive grove
      knowing these cliffs & chasms would once more shift
        & tumble down

i passed an enormous lizard being devoured among the
      shards
    by black ants hungry & mean

a bat grazed my hand at dusk a slipper moon horned
    the mountaintop

& on the plateau
    beneath olympus the chairs & tables trembled in the
      hotel
    while the tourists chewed with embarrassed whispers

      & the shopkeepers mad with greed
    plundered their hopeless cash registers

the peasants rolled in dung beneath the peeling gold
where the mosaic pantocrator glared from the ceiling
with the jealous eye of the author

      & i have heard the ass bray & the goat cough
    & the mule fart & the cats couple & bugs bash
      & the boys hiss & dance together
        & the jukebox blast the sky

but the meaning will not break
     like light
the message will not come thru

the beast cannot follow the waterbearer
       into the upper chamber
           & the time
is at hand

Delphi, ca. 1964

The Ex-Nun and the Gay Poet

For Helen

They talked about meditation,
the astral body and Extra-sensory perception
and the Lost Continent of Mu
and her eyes kept straying to the hair on his chest
where his shirt was open against the heat
and he talked of his new book of poems
and his eyes kept straying to the slit in her crotch
where her slacks were tight, gathering moisture
and she said she'd love to read his poems
and that night he got some Lebanese hash,
it was her first turn on
and she slumped a little on the couch,
slightly apprehensive,
and said, "Nothing is happening,"
and he laughed, watching her
and she said, "I feel as if our bodies
are moving towards each other
like 2 sticks in a bathtub
of their own volition,"
and he reached over
cradling her neck in his arm, saying, "They are,"
and couldn't wait to remove his pants.

That night they slid back
through movie stars and saints,
to Christ and the Virgin Mary,
Isis and Osiris,
Adam, Eve and ape,

fish and amoeba,
they went back to the cross, the circle,
the serpent on the tree,
the sacred mushroom
god, sperm and egg.

It was never quite so good again
but good enough.
He wrote poems while she spoke
of the convent in Boston
where all the nuns were in love
with the muscular dead body of Christ spreadeagled up there
on the cross, a MAN, and quite naked
and they did weird things to each
other like flicking the habit
against each other's breasts
which made them horny
and drove them crazy.
"They stank of each other's crotches," she said,
"a lot of cuntsucking must have gone on."
So she quit. Went in search
of a real man.

She went to work at the US Army Base in Libya
where she had troubled dreams of the Boston strangler
and woke up screaming because she dreamt of a man under the bed.
Then he was *in* the bed.
But it wasn't the strangler, it was a G.I.
After that a cameldriver.
And after a string of these
she felt she needed something more "spiritual."
So having read Lawrence Durrell she fled to Athens
ready to find herself. . .and a man.
But she didn't even find Anthony Quinn.
And the Greeks had nothing in common with Plato and Socrates.
They had nothing to say except "I love you 50 drachmas please."
This forced her to drown her dreams of the Strangler
in bottles of ouzo and retsina
with the male hustlers in the tourist tavernas.
But this wasn't very "spiritual."
She was losing her looks, her money, her mind
trying to find a way of giving and receiving
that was not just physical.
It might have been curtains for the ex-nun from Boston

but one day it happened,
what she had prayed for,
under the Parthenon.
"I met you," she said,
"I hit the jackpot."
At last she found her mystic union
through body and soul
with a gay American poet from Brooklyn.

Porto Santo Stefano, Summer, 1970

Zorba's Dance

Four days before we met I wrote about your features, cast of mind.
I explored the journey of your psyche, hoping for a sacred union.
The balance was delicate, like a mouth gaping in a dentist's chair.
One risks exposure, an aspect from which I have had to suffer too long.
Gipsy, Wandering Jew, Elijah, I envisaged an actual love commune.
How could I know that everyone would end in broken vows?
To shatter the silence I play a Greek dance alone in my room.
I dance around and around on a Cretan beach.
There is nothing but the sand, the sea and the sky peopled with ghosts.

London, 1967

III. CALIFORNIA
(1968-1979)

Opera House in the Sky

For Allen Ginsberg

a flock of pterodactyls picking their noses high above the snowy clouds

what gentle flight! there's Greenland down below—37,000 ft.—a continent of ice

Pot-Au-Feu, says the *Tribune de Genève,* K.O. and many other trite nothings—the hostesses *don't* smile

businessmen talk German, study indices and scribble accounts

air-conditioning and muzak clobber the senses—give me a cold—it's night tho' the sun's still shining

we're getting a bit tippy while the queer Dutch vetriloquist, on his way to the lavatory, says, "I am a very big strong sick man!"

and the Company Director passes: *Guten Tag!* everyone's so polite!

Big Mouth never shuts up for a minute, telling the world about her operations, her age, her job—it's the talking sickness, she admits, as the pained man listening chokes with anger and boredom

and she raps, "What is illness? is it real? I've thought about it all my life. Is it Mind, is it diet, is it air, is it poison, is it feeling, is it conflict, is it fear, is it not doing or not being, is it unused, misused energy? Please tell me to shut up!"

and the man smiles and smiles and murmurs softly, "I'm really innarested."

"What is illness but unused energy? energy crushed and shrunken into small clots of gray lumpy snailish matter? energy drained, siphoned away by misuse of feeling. misemotion."

"What will you have to drink?" purrs the hostess

and a potty little guru comes and croons, "There is Something Beyond!" waving his hand vaguely in the direction of the toilet—

Big Mouth looks up briefly, then back to Numb Listener: "I'll bet my guru is more tranquil than your guru!"

and a beach flashes a gang of bank crooks run by a master mind

intermingling hot kisses with white foam

and Marlene Dietrich sings *Allein in Einer Grosser Städt* followed by *Horepse Me Mas*—Dance With Us—on the earphones

while Americans play poker in shirtsleeves

and I am reading Edgar Cayce's prophecies in **EARTH CHANGES** about the break-up of the North American continent—will Los Angeles be there when I arrive?

Space and Time have zeroed into my psychic fallout mind and I watch for signs and portents flying silver birds that skim the polluted skies

tsunami will reach 100 ft. to drown our outlaw country—slavic
hordes will take over—Atlantis **RISE AGAIN**—and **MU**—the
Hopi prophecy come true—White man destroy himself, broken land
return to Red Man—

I am zapped by vibrations from 20th Century mosaic laws of
simultaneous sense perception

in this science fiction return to America—a decade and a half gone
and:

"They're all wearing their old age make-up," Judith Malina quips
backstage at **THE MYSTERIES**—in Geneva—"except you!"

welcomed by Allen Ginsberg with a quick affectionate kiss: "I'm
learning how to milk cows, I've got a farm upstate—it's like those last
drops of jissom from a cock!"

as Scheherazade and Maurice Chevalier and Steve McQueen
celebrate my return—

(in an emergency o my poems we'll go together in flame and water!)

meanwhile I'm a doctor with a stethoscope listening in on the
divine heartbeat of the planet's soulsounds

over great landmasses and vast mountains—*C'est Magnifique* sings
Chevalier—Great Moments In Showbiz—Magister Ludi—

the plane bumps—my pen moves across the page like a seismograph
registering inner shocks and tremors of thought and feeling

speeding thru space toward President Arch **CREEP**—ah, there's
Carmen taking over the Presidency, thank God! any smuggler band
would make a better state than our killer govt. infecting the world like
a cancer

with William Tell's pastoral sweetness before the storm

vapors clouds brown soil erosion—I'm an astral doctor—my
musical stethoscope diagnosing Earth's ills—it's cancer I tell you!
America eaten away in a kind of badlands virus disease of redneck
greed!

I look at sulphurous gold we float above like gods—Fasten Your
Seat Belt! Attachez Votre Ceinture!

great wasteland never seen on European continent! and now Verdi,
Prelude to Act III La Traviata—all periods and sounds, all places and
spaces merge—at the Opera House in the sky! violins! bel canto!

we taxi down into manic Manhattan of my birth and related
mysteries!

Geneva/New York/Venice, CA, 1968/71

Gone with the Wind

I wake in the dark aching
Alabama! I can hear
old Mrs. Mitternight
in the sheet metal yard
at the rolltop desk
looking down from the wood railing

"Son, it will hurt
a whole lifetime—"
(the deep McBurney incision)

and it did, the war wound
a whole lifetime

In the Catholic hospital
with the crucifix over the bed
the horny nurse peeked
under the sheets:
"Whut y'all doin', huh?"
exploding in giggles
and she wasn't looking
at my appendix

Southern jokes in a gray ward
always about peckers
—stitches of laughter
and clamps over the drain
biting into cut flesh
yards & yards of gauze
with pus

"Handsome" they called me
until I stood up
then it was "Shorty"

and the old guy tottering
out of bed in the ghoulish
glare of sick dawn
couldn't be kept down
because death was upon
his huge bald head

and I heard for the first time
the death rattle

*

The midget and weightlifter
shared the same room—weird freak combo
of muscle and mite—

"his mouth
jest on a level
with mah fly—"

and in the steamy Mobile night
I saw the midget blow
the hot weightlifter
spittle gleaming
at the corners of his lips

*

Mr. Nil reading Rupert Brooke
belching
at the Alabama Shipbuilding Co.
where I wore a helmet
and muddy boots

and saw a black man
beaten to death
one blazing noon
fists and lead pipe
crashed into his skull
till his face went
beyond pain
MURDER! I yelled
"Shuddup!" they snarled
"or we'll lynch ya too!"

no one believed me
"It never happened!"
said the news desk editor
with an icy stare

*

The governor's daughter had a green Lincoln
and a dogface—
at the mansion I was eligible
tho' the guv didn't believe me
when I talked of what I had seen
at the shipyard
500 white men gone mad
he preferred talking "classical music"
(Dance of the Sugarplum Fairies)
genteel Old South Monticello image

The guv headed a grocery chain
his wife was a pretty brunette
they had a French name
it was all peachy
but the daughter had a dogface

"Haow curm yew so blaaack?"
one of his kids drawled—
"Not black," I said, "dark—
sunburned—but your old man
is *real* black!"
if that's the word they wanted—
reason weaker than blindness
especially in a fine old Gone-With-The-Wind
mansion with corinthian wooden columns &
"darkies" in white jackets
(like a whiskey ad)
to serve us
smiling (only they didn't
smile—they looked
frozen)
everybody looked frozen
in some kind of deepfreeze
of the head

and back at the sheet metal yard
bewildered sharecropper fellow-workers
spat on the ground
scratching their nuts
unable to grasp
how I made "Southren sassiety"
and me just another apprentice

and damyankee to boot
(I could have taken over the state with my looks)

but the governor's daughter
had a dogface
not even a green Lincoln
could save her
tho' she tried pushing her boobs
against me
saying Tschai cow   sky
and took me for rides
in the green limousine
and kept staring at me
saying, Doncha *luurve* Cho pin
and panted in the parlor
almost dropping her undies:
Ooh, tell me about Bee tho ven!

I preferred mammy shacks
sneaky honeysuckle sex
under wrought iron balconies
black ghetto red light nights
whisper & rustle of hustlers
raising of skirts
dropping of pants
quick! bend over!
hurry!
no   glance   back

*

I had escaped the fighting
in the Maritime Commission
among azaleas and rotten shacks
among men who knew how to hate
hate for the wrong thing
always the wrong thing
metal birds burned down the skies
out of sick visions
you couldn't run from Hitler or Roosevelt
or ratproofing
the world swarming with rats
and we ratproofing, caulking
building Liberty Ships

in the mud of the Gulf
with U-boat periscopes
like Loch Ness monsters
Nazis off Galveston
and Mobile
as we made the world safe
for vested interests

*

my cut side ached
and the blond kid I roomed with
drove us to "niggertown"
where the laundress made us wait
on the old batch. we hadn't noticed
the sunset
or gray shadows. in the dirt
and gravel
of a rundown funky bar
stood some young blacks. something
zoomed across the road at us.
"Bad news!" whispered the kid. I bolted
holding my right side. the kid
had disappeared. it seemed
I wouldn't get too far
without my guts all over
the street. I heard the black boys
closing in. a hand shot up
before my face. a streetlamp glowed
in my eyes like a third degree.
"a quarter, whiteboy, and yew pass!"
I dig in my pants, fish out two bits
and put it in the black man's palm.
he grins at me. with a theatrical
sweep of his arm he waves me on.
I found the kid's car just
as he was getting in, the
black boys about to jump us. I
don't recall
what happened to the laundry.

*

the first night in the boarding-house
the landlady puts me
with a fifteen-year-old boy.
I couldn't sleep. wanted to duck
under the blanket. he kept
thrashing and flailing, his legs
all over mine, one hand
grazing my belly. next night
she puts me with the blond kid: his
hairy legs remained on his side
of the bed. two nights later
it's his brother, the
handsomest boy in Mobile.
good Southern Baptists, both.
did sex exist?
I end up with a limping Spanish clubfoot,
the only ugly boy in the shipyard. we're
so horny that when he presses against me
we squirt and fall asleep.

*

in the steamy room with the blond kid
and the weightlifter, three of us,
each in separate cots, I hear
a strange flapping sound, starting
and stopping. the moon rises
over the weightlifter's cot and I see
his naked muscles white as marble
in the moonlight, his hand flapping
...starting and stopping...
the blond kid snores and I stare, making
no sound; the full moon reveals
the weightlifter's superb physique,
glowing fantastically. I creep
toward him like a ghoul, stealthily,
my hair over my face and whisper, "Warren,
Warren," hoarse with excitement. he
makes no sign of having heard
or seen me. with the wild
courage of desperation I reach
to touch him and he starts, his body tense,
glances at me, shifts his gaze
back to his burning moonlit cock
and I know it's all right.

*

Warren's asleep and Bud, the blond kid,
wakes and whispers, "Come here," and
I can't believe my eyes for he
is naked and erect; he grabs my head
and I go down. almost at once
he comes like a bull. then:
"Don't *ever* do that again, hear?"
"Didn't you like it?" I ask, incredulous.
"We don't like cocksuckers in Alabama," he says.
"It's a crime against Nature."
"It *is* Nature! You *wanted* it!"
"Never mind!" says Bud, getting feisty.
"Jest stay in yore own bed, hear? And leave
Warren alone." "That's Warren's business!"
"It's mine. If I catch you touching him
it'll cost you your job!"

*

In the Bellingrath Gardens
gray Spanish moss hung
from live-oaks in hazy tresses.
The scent of gardenias
came from beyond the boxwood
borders. A brown thrush
fussed among dead leaves.
I stood on a parterre overlooking
the broad lake; behind me
splashed a fountain into
a marble basin. My brain sluggish
I felt the moss envelop my senses
in the grillwork plaza with strange
iron benches, forgetting ugly
dumps, crumbling shacks,
shipyards, factories.

*

In China, Europe, Japan, the war.
Here, the shipyards, the airplane factories.
My nerves beat, drilled and hammered,
they pounded and tapered and punched,
they ratproofed and sheared. They steamed
with the loud exhaust from the gantry crane.

They hissed and rumbled with the clam-shell bucket.
They hooted with the locomotive, screamed
with the buzz-saw. My nerves
made a vast fire
in the stoke hold of freighters,
blazed in the furnace, smoked through the stacks.
I lost myself in blueprint and steel.

*

The old Chief's balls hung down to his knees.
Even the jockstrap couldn't contain them.
We laughed like hell when he stomped around
the flat we shared, growling and grumbling,
his balls swinging like some tired old bull's.
We were the young ones and joked
about everything, but mostly
about the old Chief's balls.

*

At Dr. Terrell's on Royal Street
a fat young man painted
"lahk Picassio," had thinning
fair hair and washed-out blue eyes
and an unpleasant habit of grabbing
my head and shoving it down
to his crotch. I forced back his hands
each time and would have slugged him
but he was too soft and would spatter.
He'd whip out his thin
purple dick and jack off, hoping
to elicit some response. But
a dog would have been more tempting.
"Picassio" stopped talking
only when he masturbated. He rode
the streets in an old Ford shouting
obscenities at blacks when he got drunk.
Dr. Terrell shuffled home
and sat in the old library drinking,
exchanging a few words with "Picassio"
and glaring at me as if the Civil
War had not yet ended and
I was a spy in the house.

*

Around the dead frame of the house
the street fell down below the gate.
The garden smelled of fish and roses
where centuries of pet cats ate.

What happened in the library
before the wind blew through the glass?
Coming back each night he sits
whispering "Frankie" as the hours pass.

Each night he shuffles up the porch
as pillars shake and dry wood creaks,
prepares his dinner, doffs his hat,
and ritually, softly speaks:

"Frankie! Frankie!" to the books
in faded jackets on the shelves.
The Twenties thrillers, loose romances
fail to implicate themselves.

Silent as the chokecherry leaves,
old Ambrose in the kitchen knew
his mistress when she lay and read
two lazy decades lightly through.

He hears the doctor whispering
the catechism of her name.
The evening sighs on Royal Street
like ghosts that drape the mansion's frame.

Now Dr. Terrell's dead; his gun
that never once had left his hip
cannot be questioned, nor the house
and Ambrose with the buttoned lip.

*

A cold wind blows through the world.
The West decays and crumbles.
The East destroys the Soul.
The threat to life grows greater.
The century wanes,
the world shudders.
Love alone pleases the Soul.

All the rest is waste.
Lechery, venery, sex, lust.
All the rest is waste.
Gay, bi, kinky, straight.
All the rest is waste.

Heidelberg, 1967/Venice, CA, 1970/San Francisco, 1976

Let Me Love All at Stillman's Gym

freakshows. ferris wheels. rollercoasters. glittering thrash of surf. sea-
smell. saltair. youths in openair lockers. sand. sun. nude bodies. they
look up and see me in toilet window. they make obscene Italo hood
gestures. up yours. *va fongool.* left hand pumping bicep in crook of
right arm. shame. I blush with shame. they think I'm a girl! crimson
shame. I'll die of shame. and delight. excitement pumps hot blood
through my veins. chestnut hair over my eyes. I can see my bangs glint
coppery red in the sun. everybody looks up at me. my cheeks and lips
burn. they must be flaming red. I peek over the bathroom window
ledge. *Hey! ya want dis?* they yell laughing. mocking yet sweet. they
grab their dongs and wave and waggle them half-hard. their hips press
forward. hump the air. *Come 'n' git it!* HAHAHA! sparks shoot out of
my hair my skin. I am full of electricity. I grab the toilet paper
cylinder. slide it in. pull it out. they can't see. they make farting lip
sounds. the razz the Bronx cheer. *Hey kid wanna wop salami? c'mon
down!* they collapse with laughter. slap each other's suntanned muscles.
bend their knees on the sandy floorboards of the showers. helpless with
excitement. lustful laughs. they gleam gold. dance under the shower
spray. wet. hot. salty. sea and sperm. froth and foam. salt of the earth
and sea. *if the sandman brought me dreams of you.* I pick one out with
my eyes. tall. lean. ample cock. he looks up. defiant. provoking.
tender. sneers like a bully with feigned contempt. then slyly winks.
(buddies do not see this. they see only the sneer.) then secretly points
forefinger to breastbone. then points at me. together. us. him and me.
I'm suffocating. scared. tantalized. breathing hard. what shall I do? I
hide behind Auntie May's chintzy white toilet curtains. *I think I'd
dream my whole life through.* minutes later I peer furtively over the
ledge. they have forgotten me. nobody looks up. I feel lost. suddenly
unwanted. they slap each other's butts. grab dicks. flick towels. yelp.
make dirty gestures. yell with hoarse teen voices. sneak looks in my
direction. pretend not to notice me. I flush again. I can almost smell

the musk from their bathing trunks drying on sandy floorboards in the sun. the seabreeze wafts the musky odor in my direction. I feel faint with lust. they whistle. piercing. loud. tongue curled between the teeth. they slap each other hard. smacking sound. flat hard palms against flat hard bodies. they whip wet towels across butts with a smart crack like a gunshot. cackle. shadowbox. prance. HAHAHAHAHA. they do not look up. should I go downstairs? what will they do? call me dirty names and beat me up? I could not stand it. the one I love looks up. loud Bronx cheer with puffed out lips. then sneers handsomely. waggles it. long. thick. pointed. foreskin. lips curled. arrogant. beautiful. *for you brought a new kinda love to me-e-e-e. . . .* I duck. I hide. rouged with shame and desire. it's too much. in medicine cabinet mirror I see my face. like a girl's. roses and olives in my cheeks. flash of brilliant teeth. I grind them in agonized frustration. Calcium they call me at school. my teeth so pearly white. Handsome Harry they call me. pubic hair thick and shiny. and new. I am 13. I watch the young men under the silk spray. twenty-eight young men bathe by the shore. they do not know who watches and loves them. behind the curtains I make love to America. in the closet I make love to America. my love is bigger than the Atlantic Ocean. America does not want my love. America throws sand in my eyes and tries to drown me in the Atlantic Ocean. but my love is bigger than any ocean. over the greatness of such space steps must be gentle. everywhere sand and waves and sun flashing. superb young acrobats in tank suits. they build a throne of bodies. along the sand I crawl on my belly to the throne. I am a slave to the monarch of flesh. no god more precious than this throne of youth. let me love you all at Stillman's Gym. I am 13. I want to love America. America with its smell of gymnasiums and locker rooms. America with its smell of hamburgers and hot dogs. America with its smell of jockstraps and privates. America with its deodorants and disinfectants. America laughs at me. Steeplechase laughs. Luna Park laughs. the fat lady jellyrolls and laughs. the seal boy with black flippers laughs. Zip the pinhead laughs. multitudes on the beach laugh. under the boardwalk the lovers laugh. the bank director in a beach cabana eats the newsboy's ass and laughs. a great horseshoe crab rots on the sand with slimy maggots infesting its jurassic head and laughs. I poke it with a tarry stick. it dissolves into the sea's endless rhythm and laughs. I fade out in dumb relentless seasurge. I do not laugh.

*   *   *

fingers delicately palpate hairs on backs of thighs

run gingerly along bulge of buttocks

rest gently on asshole

belly trembling—bands of muscle ripple—

suck in—waist tight—thighs arch—like bows—

arrow ready from quivering tendons

to shoot—

lower my head and grasp my feet—

tickle my toes with moist fingers—

bend down further—straining—

back and spine aching—

lips purse with kissy stress

towards pearly glistening moisture—

heart pounding—tongue darting—

hands clasped beneath thighs—

grappling—bending—snout burrowing—

pressed in musky nest—

aaahh! mmmmmm!

GULP!!

Venice, Calif., 1969

When Law is Murder

"If the government becomes a lawbreaker it invites every man to become a law unto himself; it invites anarchy."

—Supreme Court Justice Brandeis

He took ginseng & mu tea,
worked out with weights
and resembled an anatomical chart.

He was not a monster on display
but a nice blond kid
at Muscle Beach.

He reached down
to a paper bag
& gulped some dago red
without removing the bottle.

"I've been drinking it all day,"
he said. "Helps me thru
a workout." He winked
and I felt a bolt of love.

Then I saw it, from
the underside of his biceps
around to the triceps. Worst
goddam burn you ever saw.

"Didja notice the pigs in the prowl car
waiting to catch me
taking a drink?" He took another.
Spat. "I'm 26, just back
from Nam. Legs burnt
by fire-bombs. Now
they want me to be a good boy,
no drinking, no screwing. Does
that make sense?"

His sinewy tanned back gleamed
in the sun. Everyone
wore bikinis, bathing trunks.
He never removed his pants.

Venice, CA, 1969

Mr. Venice Beach

The gym stank of armpit and crotch and male ego,
the hustlers with their golden boy good looks
strutted as usual, powerful and lazy with muscle,
throwing Mr. Universe poses and sipping honey
from plastic bottles or raw milk between sets.

The competition was coldblooded and the conversation
hard edge, about who had the biggest pecs
and were Rick's abdominals more cut up this year
and did Joe really get 200 bucks off the faggot
who phoned the gym from Pennsylvania
clear across the country, just for a date with him?

Charlie was throwing poses in the mirror
like a contest winner, raising his huge arms
over his tiny head and flashing a Mr. Big Biceps shot
and then a fast latissimus in the old John Grimek style.

Then Charlie quit taking immortal stances
long enough to come over and say, as he wiped the sweat
from his obliques, A funny thing happened on my way to the
gym at the Federal Building in downtown L.A.
This car comes charging up the road onto the curb
and crosses the grass and smashes into the building,
and when the cops get there they find this note:

I'm across the street in the cemetery, dead.

They found the guy there.

Then Charlie started back to the mirror.

He placed second in the Mr. Venice Beach contest,
he said, flexing his quadriceps.

Venice, Calif., 1969

The Queer-Killers

Kick the fag in the nuts. Bash
out his brains; they're not
doing him much good. He's a loser,
a queer. Break the fag's
goddam ass. Shut his cock
sucking mouth for the last
time. He's a pervert, a sick
degenerate. Break his face.
The law won't touch us, chum.

Venice, Calif. ca. 1970

A Warm November Afternoon

in the sun on a warm
november afternoon a vast
synthetic paved square
with a fountain from which
poisoned city water flows
it's the Embarcadero
Plaza & I'm flat
on the curved cement benches
thoughtfully laid out
for the recumbent human form
by the recumbent city planners
thoughtful but not aesthetic
& businessmen in money uniforms
rigidly walk by with short hair
mad-looking among the freestyle young
they pass with scarcely a glance

the kids mostly black &
brown scream & play
splashing in the water
while 2 young men beside me
dart furtive glances at my bare
hairy aging albeit muscular
torso as they munch
lunch
always these signals of restless
quest for ecstasy, freedom
under the humdrum externals

as life goes on
secretly beneath the noise
and speech that exist
on broader daylight terms
of falsity

San Francisco, 1971

Harley-Davidson

I climb on the Harley-Davidson
behind him. "Hold me," he says,
"around the waist!" my arms
petrified as we hurtle through Brooklyn.
he glances over his shoulder.
to show appreciation I smile, thighs
numb with tension. the feel
of his lean belly under the leather
is soothing. Nick's slant
blue Russian eyes sheathed
in the Jaeger like that scene
of Slavs and Teutons on the ice
in Alexander Nevsky, he turns
into a knight, I his vassal.
we ride the lancing air,
one with the machine
alive and leaping, sailing
a concrete sea. words
had not brought us together, words
made us "comrades". we never spoke
intimately. teenage marxists.
slum intellectuals.

                we shoot
by dazzling shores, roar
at the rocks—then back,
I pry loose. Nick grins,
removes the Jaeger. lank
blond hair over high
cheekbones. "Were you
scared?" still trembling I frown.
"Nah. Let's do it again next Sunday."

San Francisco, 26.vi.72

On Riverside Drive

Under the Soldiers & Sailors Monument,
under Grant's Tomb, the pulse
of a city beats in the blood
of the boys cruising each other,
the trees & shadows give off
a sexual feeling, benches
extend a promise; rank
odors of leaves, damp
mulch of groins; they expect to
find each other after hours,
after the opera, the ballet,
after Lorca and Whitman and Stein,
after whiskey and Billie Holiday,
after everything has closed down
and the night is about to begin.

San Francisco, 9.v.72

I am Going to Fly Through Glass

For Anais Nin

Perhaps you do not remember the effervescence of the Rumanian
girl in church waiting, it is true, for a mortician in groovy tennis shoes
perhaps it was so much like everyone, but more pederastic, the
love I pretended when you were tearing the iridescent neck and the cab
left the respectable houses farther down to where the crews were
displacing the river
in the darkness we became even more aware of the Doctor who is
soft as a bat in the green night...the narcotic fireworks... the softness
she felt as she swallowed some of it...the inside smelled of sandalwood
I have lost count of the years of darkness, with the keen knife I cut
the first throat I saw, I cannot lament the loss, and o, the night pleases
us like memory
I'm busy writing a fantasy in verse to forget the victim who fell
before the Cross, in vain trying to convince himself
I remember you danced in the labyrinth when I was tormented in
different parts of the city fighting so many things

then I could do nothing but submit to a cruel dream...I saw trees
move intravenously and flow through passageways where I appeared
disguised as many faces and

entered a room whose walls smoked, burnt letters fell like onion
skin, in Gothic script

at the top of the staircase a woman thrust her breasts sensually
forward, struggling out of a chastity belt, and devoured the wallpaper
depicting a muscular equilibrist in orange tights whose head resembled
one of mine

my jaws ached, I had been grinding my teeth in the underground
laboratory where the "King of the World" ruled...I held in my hands
a crown of feathers...I could hear gold...music poured through my
fingers...I am going to fly through glass....

San Francisco, 1972

Dreams

Tell me, dreams, will I find a new lover?
How do you feel, dreams, about my taking a new job?
What are my chances, dreams?
Will I get rid of my backache? will my luck change? will I travel?
    become famous?
Dreams I want to know. I have given you my best years and what
    have you given me?
I sacrificed everything for you, placed you on an altar,
    invoked your images, burned my bridges for you.
I whispered of you to my best friend. I followed where you led.
I consulted you, took dictation from you, I was a faithful servant.
    I listened reverently when you spoke, obeyed when you
    commanded, studied your moods.
I puzzled over your riddles, divined your symbols.
Nobody has trailed more closely in your wake.
I saw decayed interiors, stone mazes, wild horses plunging into the sea....
I went through outlandish metamorphoses.
How have you rewarded me for my fantastic pursuit?
Come on, dreams, let's level with each other!
I am just where I stood at the start of this journey, dreams!
Brrrr! oh fucker! this thought scares the piss out of me!
I mean, everything I've thought and done, dreams, *everything* has
    been thru you, and now you're leaving, walking out! I'm getting
    older, more tired, catch cold easily, and, worse,

growing forgetful, not remembering you! this is dangerous. . . .
Don't, for god's sake, leave me, dreams! You're all I've got.
If you go nothing's left, only the dull puke of everyday "reality"
that dreamless gloom! Glub! I'm drowning! shopping and dollars!
election speeches! dirty laundry! kitsch! schlock! AAARGH!
pollution. statistics. data processing. shriek. racism. computers. gulp.

taxes. war.

I'LL THROW UP!! Don't leave me, dreams! I'm nothing
without you. . .shit. . .just shit.
You're my everything, dreams, my oracle my guru my divine right. . .
my cock my cunt my year-round asshole. . .my boy my joy
my cookie my nookie my groovy suck!

San Francisco, 21.ix.72

This Has Been Happening a Long Time

For Gerard Malanga

someone very familiar
tho' we've never met
fumbles around with his tool
shed while I crouch beside him
I request machine oil
for my squeaky bicycle
he hands me the oilcan
I notice his black velvet pants
with a flower design
our pants are identical
I reach up to tell him
with my hand that caresses the soft
material under which the hard
teenage thigh grows
more familiar
my hand explores his calf
the muscular buttocks and
something swelling in front
my mother calls Lunch Is Ready
he may be the brother I've wanted
we chat like blood relations
comfortable with each other
my mother rides a snow sleigh into the kitchen
she is having her problems

we laugh at her worries
we share an inner knowledge
he responds to my touch
with no visible emotion
I am growing upset
I reach for his penis
I hold it like an electric eel
electrons come in my hand
he seems to melt into the snow
and sound of sleigh bells
this has been happening a long time

San Francisco, ca. 1972

I'm Not a Man

I'm not a man. I can't earn a living, buy new things for my family.
I have acne and a small peter.

I'm not a man. I don't like football, boxing and cars.
I like to express my feelings. I even like to put an arm
around my friend's shoulder.

I'm not a man. I won't play the role assigned to me—the role
created by Madison Avenue, *Playboy,* Hollywood and Oliver Cromwell.
Television does not dictate my behavior. I am only 5 foot 4.

I'm not a man. Once when I shot a squirrel I swore that I would
never kill again. I gave up meat. The sight of blood makes me
sick. I like flowers.

I'm not a man. I went to prison resisting the draft. I do not fight
when real men beat me up and call me queer. I dislike violence.

I'm not a man. I have never raped a woman. I don't hate blacks.
I do not get emotional when the flag is waved. I do not think I should
love America or leave it. I think I should laugh at it.

I'm not a man. I have never had the clap.

I'm not a man. *Playboy* is not my favorite magazine.

I'm not a man. I cry when I'm unhappy.

I'm not a man. I do not feel superior to women.

I'm not a man. I don't wear a jockstrap.

I'm not a man. I write poetry.

I'm not a man. I meditate on peace and love.

I'm not a man. I don't want to destroy you.

San Francisco, 1972

Underground Love

old man mutters under dogwood
as 3 straight suited exec types
cross the street looking brainwashed
i.e. stiff prejudiced unloving
their money uniform looks wooden
cars flow by to freeways
Oakland hills like Fiesole
Tuscan panorama from downtown San Francisco
I've left part of me in Tuscany
part of me in Sicily
pieces left in Rome Paris Tangier Athens NY
with boys in the international
underground of love

San Francisco 2.iii.72

Reading My Poems at Universities

reading my poems at universities
dazzled and stimulated
by muscular bare legs on campus
hairy young studs and clean-cut smoothies
when will I fill this sexual void
audiences just waiting to get at the liquor
I dazed and wandering among them
supposedly free and loose

not drinking
not pinching asses
not groping crotches
the very model of an asshole
I want them to come to me
(delusion of grandeur)
I'll read that book on self-hypnosis
become a rampant bard
yelling: Down with your pants!
ah you creep, when will you tear the locks from the doors!

San Francisco, 3.iii.72

The Bus

the bus lurches
thru underground transit co. construction zones
faces tempt me thighs make me giddy
PLEASE HOLD ON SUDDEN STOPS ARE SOMETIMES
                                          NECESSARY
what is poetry? BIT OF PARADISE DISCOUNT STORE
will I see you again?
FOR LEASING INFORMATION CALL AGENT
I think of you
HAROLD'S TERMINAL DRUGS
this is where I get off
but I don't get off
I think of a Mediterranean landscape
the twang of a Spanish guitar
sugarwhite walls
SORG PRINTING CO.
your legs are on my mind
oh, he hangs on to the strap
sneaking looks in my direction
I need him
I want to smile
he wants to smile
but he doesn't
he frowns
looks out the window
looks back at me
why don't I smile

I pretend I'm thinking
we lurch
towards somebody unattractive
ooops
the driver must be nuts stopping like that
smile goddammit smile
there that does it does what
he looks scared embarrassed
doesn't smile
and this IS where I get OFF
now he's waving he's waving at me!
now I smile now he smiles now we smile
now he looks rueful but glad
to show his feelings
as the bus speeds on

                    San Francisco, 25.iii.72

Chicken

my legs? oh
they just came
naturally big

I'm training
for
the football team

I gotta lotta
endurance
(hot
looks in the direction of

middleaged
ass
in the grass

dark blue
circles
under his young
eyes)

I'm in shape
from running
(built like a
sinewy Renaissance
puto, ripe
Italian buttocks
smelling of
parmigian')

I oughtta
be big
all over when

I'm 17

San Francisco, 18.vii.72

We Do Not Speak of Love

For Alix Geluardi

we do not speak of love
but all are pushed & pulled
by it

taking all forms & shapes
twisted pounded burnt
by it

like sculptor's clay our faces
punched & pinched
made long or ripped apart
by it

eyes pained or deep or lost
lines cut in cheeks & foreheads
from it

we do not speak of love
our faces scream
of it

haunting bars &
running wild in streets
for it

we do not speak of love
but spike warm veins pop pills
burst brains with alcohol
for it

gods & demons wrestle for the heart
of it

I can't survive the lack
of it

San Francisco, ca. 1972

Remembering Paul Goodman

1

As I cross a windy streetcorner
waiting for a bus
that never comes
in the wind and the rain
I remember
how Paul walked
with a shaggy dog trot
and half-shy smile
pipesmoking
toward a drunken party
where he ran
to hard young bodies
and handsome faces
tho' loss of balance disgusted him.
People fell
into the bathtub, smashed
and Paul stood as if amazed
at the madness of crowds.
And I recall once
when he stood at his window
sight-translating

Our Lady of the Flowers
how his blue intellectual eye
kindled suddenly
at a passing navy ass
and as he brought a criminal beauty
out of the French language
a revolver went off in his mouth
releasing
orgasms
of
light.

2

Now he does not exist
those parties are gone
the nights the lovers
gone
only the feelings remain
another here
another now
the written word will survive
somehow
in somebody's memory
this is the truth of poetry
to make it new each lifetime
Pound's gold standard of letters
Goodman's bitter faith

I write to make myself real
from moment to moment
how else do I know
I exist
if I didn't I'd go
mad with emptiness
and boredom I confess
Paul Goodman
helped us live
in the present
tense

3

Strange to hear your voice
disembodied on tape
lecturing at universities
over the air (and you're dead and gone)
less bitter than 20 years ago
some say more bitter
but you were diffident then
and shy
needing the sweet turned neck
and ear of the young
you pursued love and fame
for what? towards what?

    Lonely old Orpheus
      Romantic woodsy Wordsworth
           anarchist Shelley of coldwater flats
        on your bicycle over the bridges
           loving the pastoral urban scene
      dashing to handball courts for quickies
           blowing the boys
    in parking lots and doorways
    with Puerto Ricans on stoops
        secret jackoffs on East Side roofs
    with shepherds of chance on streetcorners
      among traffic horns and coffee smells
          smells of urine and sperm in sacred latrines
            bus stations, bars, penny arcades
          42nd Street grope movies
          smoke and kisses
O Empire City!
        Soul-brother Socrates
          tugs at your elbow—
            Catullus declaims: *pedicabo ego vos*
              et irrumabo....
        You lived in sad neglect
          till late success brought dollars
            gray hair and heart attacks—
        your son Matthew dead at 20
            your wife Sally once applecheeked
              growing old....

You wrote *The Facts of Life*
and we read our poems and joked
and met Edith Sitwell, noble scarecrow dyke
with birdlike mask
and Jean Cocteau signed copies of OPIUM
and *The Eagle Has Two Heads*
saying,
        "These English words...these are not my words...."
and flirted with me
and you were jealous
biting the stem of your pipe as if it were the pin of a grenade....
And when I said you were our Sartre everyone looked uncomfortable
                                       in 1945

but when you died the other day
a famous critic called you that
and I bought *Hawkweed* for a dollar
and read those kinky poems again
—a voice unique and personal
caught as in rock for future years!

4

Patchen's slow death of bitter pain
    Jarrell stepped in front of a car
Sylvia Plath stuck her head in the oven
    Delmore Schwartz OD'd on booze
O'Hara struck by a beach buggy
Berryman highdived from a bridge waving
    Blackburn went by cigarettes
      & Goodman forgot his pills
these are the poets of my generation
    give or take a few years
Paul's poems kept growing bleaker
    with indignation & rage
    with every sleepless night
that went without love as age crept up
    who's next? the pattern's old
freaks of the western wilderness
between the bughouse & the bar
American poets live their lives
    some starve tho' you may not hear it
    others vanish into academe
to sugarcoat their hell, grow dull
    Paul with his "pretty farm"

tried the Horatian life, it didn't work
    in a black flag he draped his love
tobacco, wrong food, loneliness
    stopped his heart the American way

5

Writing *The Glass Menagerie* was no cinch, Tennessee.

"It's only a potboiler!" he said. "Wouldn't you rather see my poems?"

Julian Beck spoke of Gertrude Stein and the revolution of feeling.
He raised black flags in hell
and threatened the world with peace and saintly patience.

Jimmy Baldwin emerged from 5 a.m. mist into neon cafeterias
with watchcap and desperado eyes
placing his naked soulscript in my hands, his negritude,
and we had to choose bars carefully.

Paul Goodman sat on my floor listening to Auden—
their first meeting—both thought they were Shelley—

Ginsberg, high in the subway, red kerchief round his neck,
recited Rimbaud in eerie dawn of 1944
drowned by the IRT, flood of words across the aisle from me
and then departed for mad mindmusic after we greeted the future.

Death, sex and war...sailors everywhere...
jukebox romance of South Sea guitars...
we cruised the salty seas of love....

I recall it all
through a scrim of decades
and broken love affairs
and rubble of dead friendships.
Paul was not sentimental:
"I do not eulogize dead men," he said.

I find that fitting.

San Francisco, 1972

A Kind of Immortality

Scientists predict that California will have a major earthquake of
devastating proportions sometime within the next few decades. Now is
the time to prepare yourself, your family and your home for such an
event. *Do not rely on others,* it is your responsibility to be prepared. A
major earthquake will tax local government and emergency response
agencies, probably beyond their capability. It is imperative that each
citizen be prepared for such an event.

—Pacific Bell Family Plan

1

I always thought
it would be like this
like my dream long ago
of great tides hurling
upon the land
myself engulfed
with struggling masses
screaming
choking
fighting
for air

now this strange
prophetic dream
seems true
as I watch the waterpipe
shaking
and the lamp on the night table
and the bed
shaking
as the earth shakes
night after night
in warning

2

From wine and dope and desolation
of taverns and bus stations
with pinball machines and video games
from waiting in vomit
at some forlorn forgotten place

and time
from the tiger of memory
from the loneliness of the last stand
with blood-torn twisted mouth
crying in a stunned alley or subway
like an exposed intestine
numbed by fluorescent tubes
from the sad choked scream
behind dirty curtains
in downtown tenderloin
where alarms go off with insistence
and hysteria
from lunch counters of donuts and coffee
with closed faces of bleakness of not knowing
anybody or oneself or anything
of being nothing and going nowhere
I want you to stop
I want you
to forget terror and suicide
for one small moment
forget earthquake and heart attack
I want you to take a deep
breath
and listen
deep inside yourself
and hear
what you heard before
you came to this
place of desolation
and tell yourself
you're not alone
it's really a dumb dream
on a mean planet
and you're going to wake up
and be somebody
you always wanted
to be

3

I saw a young man in my room
strangely intimate though unknown
yet loverlike and warm.
"I know this city well," he said,

"its hills and business district.
I'm a taxi-driver, 27, been thru
the big quake, the western hill
is safe," and vanished.
Was I talking to the dead,
some astral hitchhiker
between sleep and waking?
I fell back and heard:
"It is an exceptional time
and situation."

4

Night after night earth trembles,
stars sharp over the city.
Vehicles whoosh in the streets.
Scratching my armpits in the bleak bed
I fornicate with hot youths
in my imagination.
Why not go down with grandeur
under collapsing roofs,
pancaking floors,
coiled rocks roaring,
office buildings capsizing,
land-developers foiled,
greed smashed by Nature!
Ah, what a noble death!
This will be memorable, by god!
A kind of immortality!

5

in the city forsaken by the Angels
¼ million people seek refuge.
they run in the streets stark naked, clutching
an old photograph or a drum.
buildings shake, fall down
in a heap of plaster, glass and concrete.
in a matter of seconds bridges buckle,
cloverleafs contort, freeways tangle,
dams burst, water rushes over suburbs,
old ladies weep, traffic signals
flicker insanely, children scream,
thousands die and are buried instantly.

a naked youth in an overcoat
carries a hastily-improvised sign
on cardboard: REPENT! THE END IS NEAR!
his end is beautiful and very near.
his eyes glitter, he does not speak,
golden shoulder-length hair glows
in the sun, his legs are flawless.
I approach wanting to touch him,
speak to him, thinking of
the Angels in Sodom, but he vanishes.

to go down in a heap of rubble
with 100 twisted old ladies
sour, insane, hating life
is to die in a bombed-out ghetto
with TV alone in a room
watching commercials.
to go down in a broken city
is to die of irrelevance
for a god of phantoms
in a dream of swimming pools.
to go down stupidly
in the debris of shlock and glitz
is to die of unreality.

6

Let the dogs hump in the streets
I'd do the same if they'd let me
those guardians of public morals
who fear the horrors of pleasure
more than the horrors of war

We've grown used to our daily murder
give us this day our daily dead
our daily rape, beatings, swindles
by the law-and-order boys—
their God cannot stand Love
—their God is Death

Let the dogs go berserk
running around in dog packs
biting their owners when they
come too close—earthquake—

it makes them mount each other
humping away the fear

Meanwhile we wait for the big one
that will rip off the State, smash
the City like a toy—"Is this it?
will I die?"
we know and the dogs know
and the cats and canaries and goldfish know

But it is too big, too monstrous, too
forever for the mind
to handle. . .which is why
we stay and tell ourselves—
what will be, will be—
like the sour old ladies
at the sea's edge, turning
their faces from the sun

       Venice, Calif., 1971/San Francisco, 1972

Embarcadero Y

For Erika Horn

now the real estate pigs
have sold the old Y
I'll have to find another for my workouts

no more sweaty odors, jockstraps
everyone sneaking looks at each other
suppressing hard-ons
"Hey, man, you're in shape!"
talking of sports and women

I'll miss the showers
with a view of Treasure Island
across blue water the green hills
the Embarcadero Y will fall
to the wrecker's ball
for a parking lot
skidrow winos mopped up

they'll tear down
funky bars &
burn the piers
sending black smokerings
to vanished Indians

dust and torn streets
highrises shooting up
black as the hearts of city fathers
hard as the hearts of "developers"

oh put them in wheelchairs!
push them over the roofs!
pull down the office buildings!

they have murdered the landscape
fouled the air
left us no choice

San Francisco, ca 1972

I Would Not Recommend Love

my head felt stabbed
by a crown of thorns but I joked and rode the subway
and ducked into school johns
to masturbate
and secretly wrote
of teenage hell
because I was "different"
the first and last of my kind
smothering acute sensations
in swimming pools and locker rooms
addict of lips and genitals
mad for buttocks
that Whitman and Lorca
Catullus and Marlowe
Michelangelo
da Vinci and Socrates admired

and I wrote: Friends,
if you wish to survive
I would not recommend
Love

San Francisco, 7.iii.73

Naked Men in Green Heated Water

Naked men in green heated water
float beside tropical fish
whose electric colors vibrate in a shock of black
light where greengray jelly waves
and something yellow darts through coral
Someone descends to the water
His perfect body stirs mind ripples
Eyes float on the surface
Music pours into the "minoan" pool

Striped fish are having an orgy with an electric eel
Snaky tendrils sprout
from the mouths of these young men
grabbing each other between the legs
where they explode roman candles of dazzling sperm

In this wetness feelings flower
like muffled dreams
like boats shot into the sky
like sweat mingling with tongues
like a rapist wearing his victim's skin

San Francisco, ca 1973

Mysteries of the Orgy

1

hands reach silently to touch me
mouths graze my shoulder like moths
fingertips palp my genitals
the scent and touch of my lovers
humming like moon rockets
launched into astral deeps
novas white dwarfs red stars
milky ways stream thru my breasts
white as Einstein's radium hair

my body awakes I'm resurrected I'm risen
watching bodies in stellar clusters
against the walls
in circular rhythms of planets
"each member an island universe"
I'm licked into shape again
in the darkness of this room
bodies give off light and heat
that may last a moment or lightyears

2

touching ourselves into blood's renewal
we wipe out many deaths
my soul comes when I lose myself
when I plunge into an ocean of touch
how long can I inhibit my profound empathy
without touch my feelings are twisted my spinal cord shrivels up

3

we are organisms like rivers
we are miles of flesh flowing
    towards the healing ocean of a mouth
we are seconds of a pulse
we are fields of flame
we are worlds shuddering in flight
we are unsolved murders
    committed by our secret feelings
we are corpses singing with our blood
you close my wounds with your tongue
thoughts dissolve in the meeting of lips
we wander in and out of each other
    as in unknown rooms of a hotel
the Hotel Universe where the owner
    keeps to himself
we will never understand this
powerful music shoots out of the walls
the walls that are equipped
    with Death-rays and Time-machines
and we fly out of imprisoned dreams

San Francisco, 14.iv.73

Grateful

For Robert Peters

AND I AM GRATEFUL EACH DAY
Grateful to watch young bodies hard and swift
Rushing passionately after a ball
The crack of the bat like a sexual bolt of masculine thunder
Grateful to get through bullets, bombs and vehicle crash
Grateful to survive sleepless nights of puffed eyes
Grateful for reprieve from senseless annihilation
Grateful that even reincarnation is possible
As everything in the universe is possible
Grateful for love that may come in a flash
In a twinkling you're in the dance so you might as well live
Grateful for Spring, blue skies, bare thighs
Grateful for the wind and the world and the flow

San Francisco, 10.iii.73

Old Age Does Not Happen Slowly

Old age does not happen slowly
but all at once, in the head. The body takes its time
getting there, but the mind, clinging to youth
flashes suddenly—behaving as if it were still
careless!—flashes on sagging skin, discolored hair.
If you're a woman you probably cry.
Your face is set in sour lines about the mouth
at the corners, and you've an ailment that's killing you.
The ailment is Time.
If you're a man you joke about not getting it up
so often but doing it long and slow and women like it
better that way haha and you talk about the good old days
of football and war.
But if you're gay you're dead.
Nobody wants you, old friends think you're pathetic
and leave you alone with brief visits.
You eye the beauties like some leftover dinosaur
hovering in silence, terrified
of those hard men you used to have.
For if they go with you now it may be your funeral.

San Francisco, 4.v.73

You Must Have Been a Sensational Baby

1

I love your eyebrows, said one.
the distribution of your bodyhair
is sensational. what teeth, said two.
your mouth is like cocaine, said three.
your lips, said four, look like sexual organs.
they are, I said.
as I got older features thickened.
the body grew flabby. then
thin in the wrong places.
they all shut up or spoke about life.

2

a pair of muscular calves
drove me crazy today.
I studied their size, their shape,
their suntanned hairiness. I spoke
to the owner of them. are you
a dancer? I asked. oh no,
I was born with them, he said.
you must have been a sensational baby,
I said. he went back to his newspaper,
I went back to his calves.
he displayed them mercilessly.
men stole secret looks at them.
women pretended he was a table.
they all had a pained expression.
he went on reading the Sports Page.
his thighs were even more cruel
thrust brutally from denim shorts.
the whole place trembled with lust.

San Francisco, 1973

We Bumped Off Your Friend the Poet

We bumped off your friend the poet
with the big fat head this morning

We left him in a ditch

I fired 2 bullets into his ass
for being queer

I was one of the people
who went to get Lorca
and that's what I said to Rosales

My name is Ruiz Alonso
ex-typographer
Right-wing deputy
alive and kicking
Falangist to the end

Nobody bothers me
I got protection
the Guardia Civil are my friends

Because he was a poet
was he better than anyone else?

He was a goddam fag
and we were sick and tired
of fags in Granada

The black assassination squads
kept busy
liquidating professors
doctors lawyers students

like the good old days of the Inquisition!

General Queipo de Llano
had a favorite phrase
"Give him coffee, plenty of coffee!"

When Lorca was arrested
we asked the General what to do
"Give him coffee, plenty of coffee!"

So we took him out in the hills and shot him

I'd like to know what's wrong with that
he was a queer with Leftist leanings

Didn't he say
I don't believe in political frontiers?

Didn't he say
The capture of Granada in 1492
by Ferdinand and Isabella
was a disastrous event?

Didn't he call Granada *a wasteland*
peopled by the worst bourgeoisie in Spain?

a queer communist poet!

General Franco owes me a medal
for putting 2 bullets up his ass

San Francisco, 1973

The Other

1

I am a drooling pythoness
crawling through rivers of mud on my belly
on my knees in the cosmos   on the prowl in the void
I'm the navel of the world at Delphi   I'm the oracle at Crete
back and forth on the time track   commuting through bodies and centuries
I love the taste of feet   I lick the crown of divinity
I'm the old in/out   always looking for the ONE
but finding only the OTHER

2

I'm on my back dribbling stars from foamflecked lips
in a field of flaming chrysanthemums

bizarre beasts dance
mescaline moons melt

the seal of Solomon bursts

the electric river flows

streams of holiness gush between my legs

i give birth to a white narcissus

six wands spring from the ground

lotus leaves sprout from the eye

Absolute Poem like a meteor streaks down
crushed by the Earth in a swift instant

fiery chains of rubies flood the indifferent Cosmos

i'm soaring out of my blood

3

i am a war between two madmen who never win
this weird nervous system cannot change
time or pain or memory
nibbling survival

a lunatic wailing *love love*
with all the evidence shored against me

i float on a bedsheet to the stars

the sun burns in my belly

at fantastic speed i race
to the expanding skin of the bubble
of vanishing space

i am thermonuclear entropy
running down with the universe
on a golden horn
on a seismic kick

i am a cosmic tick
living on a small cold by-product of the delicate pressure of
starlight
with a glowing anus

4

I AM AN OBELISK OF EGYPT
I HAVE COME TO CHANGE ALL THAT YOU KNOW
I'VE BEEN WAITING 5,000 YEARS
UNDER MY SCRIPTURES RIVERS DIE
PRAYERS RUST AND FLAKE
I SPEAK SYMBOLS
I GIVE OFF IMAGES LIKE SMOKE
I KEEP SECRETS
I AM ONE COOL STONE

Athens, 1964/San Francisco, 1974

Never will get used to

never will get used to
   being alone at 2/30 a.m.
restless and wide-eyed
scratching my dome and wondering where is everybody
      where's the big colorful past
   can I bring it back by meditation?
the typewriter gapes like a wound the pinups curl on the wall
Krishna blows his conch into Eternity I am the taste of water
         the Light of the Sun & the Moon
            I am the sound in the Aether
         I have a very ethnic wall
an orgy of Dutch lesbians a Chinese mandarin calendar in lacquer
                                    & gold
      a Tibetan silk tanka two Aztec lovers & Japanese calligraphy
         with a Russian May Day poster
         and I'm not feeling a bit mystic

            ah, just air from a lawn
         & trees—something I had forgotten—
myself age 15 running down the block in the wind
      a football in my arms....

San Francisco, 12.i.74

Breathing the strong smell

breathing the strong smell of each other
I want it to last forever
it is never enough
warming the coldness of the heart

we stood holding each other
two men locking eyes and lips
then your mind cut the flow
and it was abruptly over

yet I felt curiously healed
as if life were about to begin

San Francisco, 1974

The Gluteus Maximus Poem

Aha, sir, what are you fondling so fondly
    under the spray? you think you're
    unobserved but your half-hard belies
    the macho pose—and you, sir, there
    in a corner at your locker, twisting
    your rod from view under
    a towel, a stiff curved bow
    of anxious meat—and you in the steam
    room glancing over soggy newsprint,
    black and beautiful, fighting down a
    rising tool, it's no use, sweetie,
    desire will out, don't hide, let go!

In the locker room naked men sashay
    from shower to sauna with steaming skin,
    undercover agents of lust: erections
    point like index fingers
    in a mass wet dream
    where wetness ignites uncontrollable fires
    fed by dumbbells and parallel bars—
    muscles communicate like the thrust
    of missiles whose launching pad is a crotch!

The gluteus maximus is more than
anyone can stand! I'm a casualty
of powerful curves, the lissome hip,
male mounds of maddening joy!
and then those parts "men love
to gaze upon"—how to survive
flames of sinew and joint? oh god!
what butts! what beauties! bliss!

San Francisco, 10.ii.74

Dream of Frank O'Hara

I saw you being interviewed by a hysterical mob of followers
And, edging closer, got a good look at your defiant humorous face.
Quite flushed and ruddy as always, with a touch of contempt,
Only this time you didn't put me off, the haughtiness gone,
Turned to sheer madness, a venerable daft figure.
You shot answers like a ghost accustomed to being right
Coming from another sphere—yet the dead seem humbler,
Somehow, envious of us, tho' you made death a circus,
Behaved like a ringmaster, and the living who crowded you
Seemed left out of the *real* show, whose key you held so lightly.

I alone knew you were dead; the others, your "readership,"
In my dream were privileged for the first time to "see you
Plain." I was no less surprised when you chose to leave
With me, harboring no rancor for San Remo days,
Tho' I never knew why you should. We used to swap small
Talk over beer in the Fifties, eyeing the service men and crew
Cut blonds, but you were guarded, as if you had a secret
You wouldn't share. Now, leaving together, you bubbled over
With vast inspired wildness, spouting weird phrases,
The poetry of vision peculiar to schizzy types. Street noises
And pneumatic drills cut off the meaning, the city strange
Yet familiar. Cincinnati? I'd never seen it before. In a frame
House we talked to an ancient couple playing cards, you stole a jacket
And hugged it, we left, walked more paved hills, you spoke
Of violence. "All art is violence!" you said still beaming.
I was afraid, not of you but of the dimension you came from.
Our most intimate scene, this astral meeting
I can't explain, hypnotic, intense, stripped of vanity
And free of pettiness; you were never more real or living.

The whole day hung in that tricky aura of dream
And death and trivial things that you made poems from:
Notes from the street, what happened in the bar, who died
And what the cat did and who fucked whom and where you went and
Some French thrown in for flavor and all the time you're diddling yourself
With flashy rubbings from Life, gorgeous and bubbly Joy, right?

Only don't tell me that except for dreams like this
Dullness didn't drip into the spaces between sensation like Campbell's Soup,
Damaging New York, the sun, poems, music, like literary prize committees
Sitting, plop, all over your gay mood with irritating power to ignore the fresh
Imagination, so when this dream is over I'll get up and make some coffee and
Not even try to capture again the feeling of something happening.
I know that the best as in sensation happens without rhyme or reason
And I'm going to let music speak for itself for a change.

(Sure enough your bibulous rhythms have swept like giant tsunami
With the riptide of your sound through the flat surface
Of monotony bearing with a lilt of the voice and the color of orange
The drab greys and boring blues to new pinnacles of random freshness.
This dream, this death, these oneiric things, they're forms
Of my feelings, shapes of appearance, and maybe just plain mess.
But the messy earth breathes as we breathe, as animals breathe and stretch
And rush around and glow and emit sound, no need to complicate
The simple act of being that merely consists of some oxygen and flowing.)
Together for the last time, Paris, a gathering
To be patiently endured, you remarked with pinpointed
Black pupils hammering into immensity of blue clouds
In long silky skies, "All art is violence!" looking quite helplessly
Violent and angry and quite drunk, too, spreading infinite bitchiness
Like a vivid bruise in the living room made wet by bearded cocktail holders.
I retreated to NY, your first year at the Remo
Where we put away the beer with John and gossiped profoundly and lightly
Joined the Marines. You played sonarman, the juke played Elvis.
Seized with immeasurable lust at the bar I rushed through a dark tunnel
Filled with nude sailors. I heard a whirring sound. My throat
Wrapped up in jockey shorts. It was the grunt's. And patriotic.
Your saucy images collided with foregone conclusions to be gone
Much too soon for rococo joy hadn't worn out its ode.

San Francisco, 1974

In my dream, the only one I've had of Frank, it appears that my anima, in its
own tricky way, effected a gestalt, thus finishing for me an incomplete and
unsatisfying relationship with another Crab whose claws were bigger than mine.

Masturbation

1

The walls of the madhouse scream!

(witness sex starvation
scrawled in blood & sperm)

The walls are raving

      (nightmares and fantasies
in the john's eerie light
and rancid YMCA smells)

Men wander, fumble
with themselves, search
           for touch
in stoned flight that ends

      down

    on their own genitals

2

In bar or baths or street
  (oppressing ourselves)
the past stabs us with memory
it glows with that lurid
nightlight of Van Gogh's billiard table
  and Bosch's hellish scenes
    jabbed in the nerve
resonating forever
  the early memory
    stuck in the throat, locked
in the muscles, crippling
          spontaneous joy—

So
  in sleepless years of quest
    we thrust
      from one lost love
    to another

thru aching scenes
    of need

3

In Genet's *Chant d'Amour*
the young convict sucks
his own arm in the
prison cell, blows
smoke thru a straw
thru a small chink in the wall
the only physical contact with
the other prisoner; this
sends them both into
masturbatory fantasies
of each other
from which they emerge
out of woods and grass
with a single flower
dangled between
cell windows

4

The machinery of government
hides the hearts of people
from each other
Gandhi said
and so love must appear
on walls
of toilets
in letters of cum

San Francisco, 1974

Horns

For Lawrence Ferlinghetti

On the Chinatown corner of Broadway and Grant
an old man in skins and furs
with occult ornaments and symbols
is shaking a large cowbell.

In his other hand a brown lacquered staff ends in a two-pronged fork.

Around his belly a pair of bull's horns,
his fur-crowned head slowly swaying
from left to right
as in some ancient shamanistic ritual,
ceremonies out of the past.

Near him a Chinese boy locked in a deep throaty kiss with a dumpy blonde.

A white boy shoves the mouth end of a long horn
in rhythmic movements
up the Chinese boy's ass,
then blows the horn and inserts it again.

When the kiss breaks up the Chinese boy drunkenly thanks the white boy
who disappears with the still-dazed girl. The white boy's hand
grazes in quick succession four big erections
as a group of tall youths pushes drunkenly by in the tight-wedged mass.

*   *   *

I'm pressed like a piece of paper in the mob,
like a page in a book.
Bodies pass through me and I through them.
Everyone wants to burst out of their clothes,
press flesh into flesh.

The streets are lined with blow-ups of naked women in topless
bottomless shows.

The barkers scream: COME IN AND GET DRUNK AND HORNY!!

and the madness of crowds
is the madness of unreleased energy.

*   *   *

I go home with images of bodies.
I go home with the imprint of smiles.

I go home with the dry taste
and feel of untouched skin.

I go home with the flank of the cavalry horse
and the horseman's boot grazing my cheek.

I go home with the stench of the cossack's horse
lifting its tail, letting go on the crowd.

I go home with the guns from the rooftops,
the deadly control of the State.

I go home sloshing towards others,
love flooding the curbs in waves.

I go home with the iron of separation
embedded in my life.

San Francisco, 2.i.75

Thru the window
unending cars

1

Thru the window unending cars
on the freeway; downtown buildings
in dusky rush-hour light; a
single tree
redeems the landscape. Flies
buzz on the murky pane. Upstairs
the neighbor's children thump. The
blank wall of the Pacific Gas & Electric Co.
cuts off the view of Treasure Island. Under
the wall a parking lot.

2

On Mutual Benefit Life
a flag is waving; flies skid
and stagger into the room
as if gassed. Streets
are empty, everyone gone
for the weekend. Bars
fill up with single
men and women, clotted
with lonely ghosts. Loud
music and voices won't lift
the sinking stone of loneliness.

3

Past midnight.
I pad the halls
of steambaths; rock
blasts showers and TV.
I pass up orgies needing
a single naked human.
In the half-light I step
into a cubicle
and with anonymous limbs
we come together. Then
without a word we part.
I reel home to an empty flat.

San Francisco, 28.vi.75

Lost

I drove around
not knowing exactly
what part of town
this was, some tough
neighborhood
where they followed you
with their eyes. I did
a few turns, passing
cute little stucco houses
like candy boxes in the
sun, full of browns, blacks,
yellows. Finally, climbing a
long hill and taking a
turn, I
saw a gang of teenage boys
who stared with
eyes like electric
eels. Shaking a little
I slowed
down as if searching
for a house
number. My heart
beat crazily. The
kids in tight pants

ran up a driveway into
a schoolyard looking
back, laughing. I
disappeared down
the street
trembling.

San Francisco, 28.iv.76

The Big Banana

I want to liberate beautiful boys from false ideas about sex.
Sex is religious mystical healthy and nutritious.
It's like eating a banana.
The Big Banana in the sky.
I'd like to peel him and eat him, foreskin and all.
Fall on my knees and worship god's rod.
If he's Jewish or Moslem we'll eat him sliced, all creamy.
Big Banana Split with hot nuts.
Perfect Orgone Prana Orgasm.
There is no Banana but the One Banana.
All other bananas are bananas.
I am the Big Banana.
Thou shalt have no other bananas before me.
Yes, we have no bananas.

San Francisco, 1976

Playing Doctor

Cock in the ass 3X daily
and some hot cum before bedtime
was his prescription for good health.
If he missed one injection
he'd grow tense and irritable.
But at night his full firm buttocks
pressed against my prick
dissolved all tensions
in 3 or 4 hefty treatments.
Then a great softness and tenderness
transformed your features, Jim.

Like a sleepy child with tousled hair
you'd lean against me, sitting up
and gazing with enormous eyes
in love and gratitude.
At such times I wouldn't dream
of playing doctor with anyone else.

San Francisco, 12.vi.76

This Beautiful Young Man

This beautiful young man, just 20,
brings himself and his poems
lazily one afternoon
a half-hour late
recommended by a famous poet
who told me how good he was in bed.

His looks being superior
to his poems, which imitate his recommender
badly, I am kind and tolerant.
But in one poem he speaks cruelly
of how he enjoys "making old men
cry" when he turns them down.

"Ah," I say, "would you turn *me* down?"
And the little bitch does just that!
He's *straight,* he says, has a girl
and makes it with *one* man only,
the famous poet. I fly into a rage
and scream, "If I'm not famous enough for you
go fuck Walt Whitman and drop dead!"

San Francisco, 12.vi.76

Paper Bodies

For Neeli Cherkovski

1

Everything I want is in this photo of a boy, nude, completely relaxed,
his buttocks seen from a low angle shot. He stares placidly inviting and
I fade into the picture with him. I wake abruptly from a fitful dream
before dawn, knowing he is...unreality of flesh beside me in the
lonely void of a bed...(it's only a paper moon)....

2

I spend long hours gazing at you
studying all the angles

My tongue roams your body
my mouth wanders
along your belly
breastplates armpits mounds

Tongue duels with tongue
my throat engulfs you

My hands stretch out to hold
a still-life fantasy of pulp

3

Don't you want to be beautiful
like Sandow? No, the gorgeous numbers
can think of nothing but their tits
and waistlines. I'm
growing beyond the pale of their power.
They're stunning and I'm stunned, numb
with unsatiated looking. I can't eat the page
with its bevy of dramatically edible boys. But
as an old goat, maybe I *can* subsist on a diet of paper.

4

For Adrian Brooks

There's Someone out there, I tell you
who's the answer

to your prayers!
Get off your duff, Heinrich, follow
those flashing legs disappearing
on the green lawn of the city park
in red shorts. After all, it's your own
future, nein? Ja, ja, ve must go
to the next vhiskey bar
or ve must die. I tell you, I tell
you, I tell you don't ask why. A White
Line at an angle stretches along the sky
over the trees and into the roof
of the tenement across the square.
It's Election Day. We are choosing'
between horrors. I tell you
ve must die. there's Someone out there
aiming his gun at your heart.
Meanwhile on Election Day a dog is howling
in the street, mourning freedom.
Down the sloping hill of the park a black boy runs
past the sprinkler splashing the grass
and the fire engines wail chug-a-lug thru the ghetto
to another burning life. O, show me the way
to the next pretty boy
                        or I must die.

There's
Someone
out
there
I
tell
      you
            who's
                  the answer
                        to
                              your prayers
                        . . . .

He may be in a bar   or baths
                              or café
or in a bookshop
                        or on the street

He may be in a magazine

Just show me the way

                              San Francisco, 2.xi.76

To a Hustler

As Boris Karloff marches to the electric chair in The Walking Dead
    you're jacking off
But when you imitate the mating call of the Double-breasted Yellowbellied
      Sapsucker
     out on the café terrace
You attract even the local birds to the telephone wires
              who answer with bird notes of love
                because you are wild
                and free
      and scream with the sheer joy of being 20 years old
        a giant of beauty and anarchy
    and when you play the guitar and sing
You establish the live connection with pure pleasure!
        Well is it love? all
          we need is money
        You say you will support me
We could bottle the perfume of your crotch and make a bundle
        You get hard ons for TV
     that I'm no competition for
        but I could gaze at your lips and eyes
          forever
        browse in your pits
          explore those eyes
       that see only yourself
        in a child's shamanistic dream

                  There's so much to tune into
But when you break your word and lie
                    I'm unhappy
        you're breaking my trust
             and love can't survive a hustle
        watch out baby
       cool the hustler's sleazy charm
       life's a bitch
         the magic splits

Well this is a love poem
        Listen!
Joe I'm talking to you stop watching that goddam television!
      You'd stick your prick in the box if you could!
      Those cretinous phantoms
        make me puke!

Is our love Mickey Mouse?
                    don't answer that—
this is not a psychology lesson
                    it's a poem
but when I'm stoned my mind is cinema
    the universe a lousy film
            and you're playing *Magister Ludi*
            just a-hustlin thru metaphysics
                    full of weed TV and "foxy chicks"
Hey you're jacking off again!
        (even tho' you've read Alan Watts)

        I'm not Elizabeth Barrett Browning
        This isn't a marriage of true minds
        just an old hustle
        with a dash of mysticism
        ESP and a high IQ
        and you've read some Beat Poetry
        and I introduced you to Tennessee Williams
        who was grandiose and arrogant
        but all you thought about was money
        today's hip hustler longhaired and lippy
        able to talk about Siddhartha
        and pick my pocket at the same time
        a handsome kid of indeterminate sex

Well this is your friendly old poet speaking
The Good Gay Poet H. Norse who should know better
who's been around

                    Ah, but the loneliness
                        was too much
                for an incurable romantic
                        too much
                and the beauty of illusion
                Two weeks of lyrical shell game
                        was it worth it
                        yep

So thanks kid
        thanks for the trip
(Now segue to synthetic ending)

                            San Francisco, March 1976

Gas Station

The young attendant is friendly
enough but his eyes turn away
from time to time like a dog's
unable to hold my gaze for long
although we're talking about
tires and prices and I don't
make any personal remarks or
switch from a strictly macho air
yet he's uneasy an animal
instinct warning him perhaps
that he is the hunted the prey
for he has the fresh robust look
of an ordinary healthy country
boy and I long to break through
all this banal tire-talk and
whisk him off in my car to give
him what I suspect he really wants
beneath the guarded self-con
scious unease but when I
stare at his pants and see the
slight thick bulge and two
stains there he shifts his gaze
again and I'm aware that we
have got to bring the 4-ply stuff
to a close or *do* something
so I thank him and he thanks me
and I disappear to write this

San Francisco, 19.ix.76

Survivor

For D. W.

I want to make you laugh.
The long nightmare is over.
But you've stored the pain
in your narrow shoulders
and sunken chest
and small broken hands.
Survivor, child

from a Nazi camp in the suburbs
with a swimming pool
and limousines
there's nothing left
but you're still here
and I want to make you laugh.
Beaten daily till you were six
you understood
that even a brother means destruction,
that parents mean abandonment,
gone forever in the private plane
that crashed and left you in the closet
locked without food for days
as punishment for not knowing fear.
Now you're out of the closet,
20 years old
with a ruby in your right ear,
with a flowing stride and long silky hair,
with a pretty face
and an eye for men,
with a need for chains
and stinging strokes
of a strap on your rear.
But you've come through,
you're here.
Poor little rich boy,
I want to make you laugh.

San Francisco, 22.xi.76

Steppenwolves

A Sequence

1

Above The Pit

The rain tears down your defenses
slicing the grin from your teeth.
You retreat into the rainbow
colors of your guitar. Sadness of imperfection
changes miraculously into song. Clutching
the cliff of music you hang

from the notes above the pit. I come
wanting to share the sounds that transform
us, mouth snapping at love. My grin
grows back again as my lips
form words around the music
and our feelings rush
more gently into the space
from which the rain slowly recedes.

2

The Steppenwolves Are Howling

I suffer fools and madmen. This one's
invisible, magical, prophetic,
works miracles, goes
without food or sleep he says.
Muttering suicide, burning money.

All right. Steppenwolves
don't mix. But listen, kid,
delusions are a bummer. Fuck
the acid and crash. It won't
make you a rockstar overnight,
won't settle the pain. We're all
fools and madmen in our feelings.

FOR MADMEN ONLY:
the caption
of your acid notebook melts
in wavy flames on washed out pages
where the mind has vanished
like invisible ink.

3

Insomniac Dreams

You're in touch with a UFO.
You're gonna change the world.
Your eyes zap people in the street.

POWER POWER POWER POWER

I didn't know you had such power.

We move toward the edge, you throw
your childhood in my face like pie
and everything gets sticky. The mask
of madness turns into a perfect stranger
feeding your fantasies—

>   *who are you?*
extraterrestrial punk?
You threaten my life—punk talk.
A smashed nose, you say, will put
even a muscleman out—?

>   over and out.

I'm flapping in the flamy night
trying once more to reach you
but you're mad,

>   really mad—
your dreams drip on me.

When the madness breaks will you come to?

4

Rainbow Sickness

I brace
    against the greasy morning
rainbow
      sickening in the trees. It's not
the first rainbow that's let me down.
There's a pot of crap at the end.

rainbow rainbow rainbow. . .I can't
reach your blasted mind, acid
has etched out the gray, leaving
rainbow colors of a rotting fish
and it's stinking up the kitchen.
You mean harm so I cover
my ass and scream,
your loony vibes causing convulsions
instead of orgasms, turned
to a punk dream of revenge. Well, I'm
    no fantasy but if I exist
as your idea of me I can still
heft a load of reality between
your fucked-up childhood eyes

with a pitchfork
full of poems. . . .

5

Will I Ever Wake Up?

I'm dingy with dope and rain
not to mention the passionate love affair
every night with the guy in the mirror
since you walked out the door
with your 56-year-old guitar
into nonstop flights to the far side
of yourself shooting to L.A. and back

stay stoned
keep moving

across the freeway 90 mph
like your freaked-out mind
that death-defying new persona.

Junkfood can't stop you now
or the marathon of bad health.

What does the windshield whisper as you race
across California through commercials
of death?

stay stoned
keep moving

6

Disturbing The Peace

My fingers flash in erogenous zones.
The spirit of Jeffrey curls out of the smoke
into my hand. But its no fun
with no body, so bring your butch good looks back
from the other side, Jeff, I want
your legs in the mirror!
I pick up a bottle and aim it at my mortality.
My spirit sneaks up my ass
and starts feeling illegal.
Can I be busted for raping myself?

7

The Glass Bead Game

Alone in Monte Rio
where the redwoods hold their counsel
far from the magic lantern
of your french-fried brains
I don't know what to say.
Hello? It comes out wrong.
Can you hear the connection breaking
like the end of a Johnny Carson joke
the audience doesn't get?
Something shorted. Well,
thanks. Perhaps I should ask
you to step on my toes again
in the kitchen littered with bones.
The garbage bags wrapped up our scene.
All those dirty words decaying on the floor!
Your notebooks and clarinet and Martin guitar
roared in the woodstove, lyrics, old songs,
old feelings reduced to ash.
Like your driver's license, your ID.
Hello?
Is this the party to whom I am speaking?

8

Relationship

It's like Gaudí's Sagrada Familia
or Guell Park, all twisted.
It's like the tortured agonized
Jesus nailed on wood
in the dark shadows of the stone
cathedral behind the noisy plaza.

It's like the matador with his pride
as he catches a horn in the groin
and it's over, they carry him
out, with the dead bull.

*

You sit on the floor
singing, strumming
the guitar and drinking Fundador
until 3 a.m. and you lurch
to the balcony over the plaza
with the amber Gaudí lamps
and the students drinking wine
and shouting and laughing
but you do not jump
you weep and moan
saying you want to save
the relationship
that is collapsing
like the peseta and
you don't know why

*

You smile when you're angry
you go to your room and play the guitar
you bang your head against the wall
and come out with a new song:

In My Dream I Fly

In my dream I smoke
and wake up feeling guilty
my resolve broken
now the sky
has fallen
how can I
face it? but remember
it was a dream, oh my

Ah yes, I'm Adolf Hitler
Generalissimo Franco
I wake up feeling guilty
wouldn't hurt a fly
everyone's a nazi
fascist maniac
children have no mercy
adults kill and lie

I'm young rich and famous
I will never die

I have eternal beauty
in my dream I fly
I wake up feeling guilty
you stare at me intensely
despair and accusation
in your eye

I do not wish to scare
any living creature
but the monster nightmare
grows to terrify
I wake up feeling guilty
you turn into a zombie
as in a horror movie
this is no dream, goodbye

9

Love Is a Homicidal Mania

We sit looking at each other
I want to touch you
but the distance grows
    greater
and I am powerless
to break the spell of such
numbness, such bitterness
that holds us, holds us
as if hypnotized, unable
to speak or move

Finally, we look across gulfs
    unbridgeable gulfs
in silence
    waiting for the other
to speak
    no longer trusting
our voices
      our feelings
and when one of us does
speak it is about
something trivial and safe like
    what café to go to or
      what books to buy
and the abyss yawns wider

under our feet
as we yawn with boredom and
    paralysis

I cannot trust my eyes
which I keep averted
    from yours
knowing it's the end of
this deadly game
this so-called "love"

it is, at times, indistinguishable
from homicidal mania
involving 2 people who
can never be sane
around each other

We've come a long way to find
this out only to expose raw nerves, frayed
at the slightest hint of
differences
each sentence poised
on the brink of disaster

Whatever we say is wrong
we can only sit and stare
and grow paranoid
    suppressing
the need to hold each other or
    to scream

Are we forever pinned like writhing
puppets to the wall? must we go round
and round forever in narrowing
vicious circles of our own
design? If I could
answer this I'd be God
who, it seems, keeps making
the same mistakes
and even killed his own son
out of love

Homicide looks like hate
to me, but then I am not God
and do not presume to know

Barcelona/Monte Rio, 1979/San Francisco, 1985

IV. GUATEMALA
(1979)

Third World

I understand those tales
of a sick aunt you must visit
in a distant town
or a big loan you must pay *at once*

I understand your situation
those 5 quetzals are necessary
there's no denying it

But something slips
between your gorgeous body and mine
sliding across the ruins of our need

It's not us but a third
invisible body
that comes between us
    a powerful drug
that takes effect quite soon

                  Guatemala City, 15.iv.79

The Lightweight Champion
of Santo Domingo

A star among his compañeros
this handsome 20-year-old
in tight white pants

dances, talks, sings
shadowboxing under the streetlamp
outside his boarding-house

and offers himself
and the whole boxing team
of Santo Domingo

From fear and strange reserve
I hold back
although a dream is about to come true

Then wonderingly
I step
into the fantasy

Guatemala City, 1979

Rubén

You speak of large sums of money that nameless gringos send you
of 6 months in Los Angeles where you picked up your bad English
with half-shut eyes droning on about the Big Affair
the Big Love who's rich and famous who'll buy you a Cadillac
and take you to live in Hollywood and other screen romances

This evening when you lay dozing in soft gray light
in my cheap pension room near Sexta Avenida
with the born-again landlord smoking dope on the patio
as dusk fell on your nude brown body and heavy genitals
we both knew you could not rise above films and fleapit hotels
torn shoes smelly socks diesel fumes comic books horoscopes
between the parks in Guatemala City
and I know you deserve a better script (and I hope you'll get one)
than the rich and handsome gringo of your wet American dream

Guatemala City, 11.iii.79

Guatemalan Entry

Ignoring the young hot cock throbbing
        in tight white pants on my bed
how long can I go on about travel fares and news of the day?
Dark smoldering eyes, half-sleepy, half-horny, gaze at me
        from a face the color of café au lait
Guatemalan mix of indian, latino and black
slightly negroid lips with a hint of velvet purple

Suddenly I'm anxious to strip this 19-year-old down again
        and expose the rest of that dusky marble skin
    I stop talking and look at him
he comes over and presses his huge marvelous hard-on
against my face and I turn my head slightly
        to kiss his pants there

He begins to unbuckle his belt with the head of a bull
for a buckle and I smile and say *Toro*
and he smiles and says *Verdad* and suddenly
            throbbing in the room in the sun
with chocolate skin darker than the rest of him
                his cock appears

I lead him to bed where he grabs my chest under the shirt
        moving his strong hands down my thighs
that look so white and hairy against his smooth darkness
and turns me around so that my back presses against his cock
            that he pushes between my buttocks
as he kneads my nipples in the sweltering heat of the afternoon

and we both begin to hump in a tropical trance
quickly reaching orgasm, he inside me
I in my hand
            where the madness spills over
and splashes into my fist and drenches the burning bed

Guatemala City, 15.ii.79

Byron Alfonso

The dance you did in the mirror nude   erect
the ancient Mayas might have done
        or the decadent Atlanteans
before the continent slipped

                        into the sea
the pagan dance
                that bypassed time
        (ancient disco fever)

A god entered you
                as you entered me

old satyr and young faun
        sharing the mysteries
            bypassing laws

drunken-stoned temple dancer
young male whore
    reviving the ritual
        with cannabis

rubbing your smooth body
against my furry one

smell of goats and satyrs

        gleaming sweat

with each step
        and bent thigh
the god rises
        and resurrects

the grunting dance
        of erections

Guatemala City, 1979

V. CALIFORNIA
(1980-1985)

Indian Summer Afternoon

I saw him in the supermarket
  hovering above the potato chips
    and candy bars

blue trunks exposing
    smooth thighs
  beginning to fill out

      mouth
  moist and parted
ablaze with ripeness

      of fourteen years

he stood submerging
  the needs
of that flagrant mouth

in candy and chips
unnatural substitutes
  for what at this age

      nature
  obviously intended
something so pansexual

that all the taboos press
  on him
and on the onlooker

a mask of casual make-believe
  of bland indifference
so that nothing disturbs the surface

  of the supermarket
on this hot Indian summer
      afternoon

Monte Rio, 28.ix.80

Von Gloeden

1

In this Von Gloeden photo
a nude Sicilian with white headband over short black hair
poses beside a decaying wall with time-etched designs

there's a cave or niche behind him and stone seats—perhaps the
Greek Theatre in Taormina, Sicily, in the
sun in the 19th Century when the boy lived

slim hips gracefully arching from the girdle of Venus his sex like a flame
but he's dead, immortal and dead of old age long ago
yet clearly alive and young through Von Gloeden
now

2

A fountain over his shoulder a Doric temple behind
his head with vine leaves in the foreground and
a dark shadow circling his neck
chin and nose like a boy's I went to high school with
and his sex like what I imagined my friend's to be
(one summer night in the Catskills I felt it press against me
in the cabin where we slept when we were 16)

now this boy who could have been his grandfather
presses his sex through the page through space through time

3

If I could join them and the baron—all those boys
a hundred years ago! clinging to Doric columns
or Ionic columns on the Ionian Sea, flowers and vine leaves
in their hair, young masons and fishermen
clinging to maleness smooth and hard on volcanic rock and stone
forever in a holding pattern older than Greece or Rome

4

This gallery of nude photos instantly on call
grows more unreal more remote mellowed by change
a shifting sea-treasure for old men's eyes
teased out of time beyond reality's grasp

Monte Rio, Oct./Nov. 1980

Eric Heiden's Thighs

    grinning with exertion
arms flapping
            he races
      toward us from the green
          sports page
for his fifth Winter Olympics
    speedskating
             gold metal

    I wonder
      what it's like
to catch this prize
      as he skates
          off the page
      into your arms
and you remove
      his tightfitting
          sleek gold suit
peeling
      the smooth fabric
         down
      from waist
         to ankles

    jesus!
one could lie
        at his feet
look up at that godlike body
  & ask
        nothing more
    than a little water sports
(without ice
       please)

      Monte Rio, 21.ii.80

Teenage Redneck

a consciousness
lower than a
                slug's
dumb gloat and menace
in eyes and mouth

expression
like a third finger
        the letter F
blown between lower lip
and upper teeth
lingering
            obscenely

when he finishes it's

FAGGOT!

mutely mouthed

the finger's a
        .22
like the ones he empties
into birds
        and cats

hits   dead center
as he smirks
and checks this out
with his buddies

who shift uneasily
when I stop and glare
fists clenched
and stare
him down

and spit

standing my ground

his pals look
away

my eyes hold
his in a deadlock
he turns
chuckling
to his pals
they move off

I'm amazed that I'm ready/to kill

Monte Rio, 19.viii.80

The Rusty Nail

I go to The Rusty Nail
   where country lads dance
to thunderous rock rhythm

   shorts nipples baskets
   stinging odor of poppers
   cigarette smoke booze

   nothing happens
so back on   River Road
   headlights blind me
I flash   direction signal
to   truck behind
               and as I turn
into   dirt   road
         hoarse teenage voice
screams   from   truck

COCKSUCKER!!!

and   speeds   on

Monte Rio, 1980

About Time

"You *homo!*" screams the blond kid
to the little girl in the dirt pile.

They are making endless engineering
projects out of gravel
                    and dirt.
"You *homo-*
          SEX-u-
                al!"

The worst thing
                he can call her
but she doesn't cry
                or hit him.
She tries harder to please him.

The sun enters Gemini
the republic sinks into hysterics
the moon enters Pisces
not, certainly, a return
to the Good Old Days

and Venus turns her back
                          on us
while hanging in becomes
the burning question
                of the moment.

Thanks a lot, lucky stars.

Monte Rio, 6.vii.80

Double Cross

He passes the hicktown ice cream parlor
where redneck teens hang out
smiles and disappears....
he's worth taking a chance for.

I probe headlines
of newsvending machines
by the corner drugstore

and I'm just about to split
when he shows. We put out
weather reports...yes, it's
a nice day...his summer shirt's
open to the pubic rim
of his jeans...he's seventeen,
he says.

Eyes shift like gears...he's
hitching to Santa Rosa
he says with a tug
at his Marlboro
hand trembling,as he looks
toward the mountains.
Too many fags in this town
he says.

I gaze at his hot features, the vein
pounding in his throat
as he preaches
against lust and sin.
He conquers them with the Bible.
Satan he calls it. I say
I'll see him sometime
and leave him to Jesus...who scored
first.

Monte Rio, 12.xi.80

The Moronic Plague

"I believe that homosexuality should be included with murder and other capital crimes so that the government that sits upon this land would be doing the executing."

—Dean Wycoff, "Moral Majority"

A deadly dullness sits
upon this land.   A fungus
    crawls in the pits of the body
infecting the crotch.
                    It digs
deep, creating
a maddening itch and desire for release

—152—

which the disease inhibits.

                  It works its way
from brain to sexual organs
taking over completely
till nothing's left of either. But
    the patient doesn't die.

              He becomes inspired!

In the grip of moronic fever
his eyes and facial muscles harden
his heart pumps ice-water,
he throws faggots in the fire.

The sound of professors burning
pleases the Moron soul.

God speaks on television
with a country accent: "Gimme
your money, suckers! And don't forget
your property. Sign
on the dotted line."

              Electronic miracles
make the lame walk and the dumb talk.
But no miracle can make them think.

Millions fall victim to *Fungus Moronicus*.
Rival Morons shoot each other
in gangland style, warring cults from the **MORON CHURCH**
founded by Moroni, the soldier-prophet
who saw inhabitants on the moon
and sold moon real estate

              to the faithful.

When hatred erupts in plague proportions
  the religious crazies rush forth
    in great numbers
      killing everyone.

Soon everybody's dead.
Nothing but the **BOOK OF MORON** remains.
They have hurled the H-Bomb
at pornography
trashed nature
wiped out sex.

At this point in his private
viewing studio **GOD**, who
has been watching the show
without a word, yawns and mutters,
"Well, damn *Me* if this isn't the most **BORING**
situation comedy I've *ever*
dreamed up! I'm glad
it's off the air."

And that's how the stupidest soap opera
in history
lost its ratings.

San Francisco, 8.iv.81

October

You drive to the park on a fresh fall day
cloud-and-sunshine, light and dark,
paths clogged with joggers and bikes,
stealthy cops stalking gays
around soccer teams on playing fields,
in latrines and behind bushes,
through Japanese gardens and Dutch tulips.
You drive to the seashore past stone windmill
where teenage surfer in black wetsuit
with yellow surfboard like seagod appears
mellow as peach under pastel skies
over flat beach rained on the night before,
pawprints of dogs, clawprints of gulls.

Prize Afghan frolics and rolls
in sand while master cries No, No!
snatches leash with a jerk of the hand.
The Farallones like phosphorous glow,
thrust of sedimentary rock from
frothy waves. Barefoot runners
puffing dash among cracked seashells
as white yacht among white sails floats.
Black man with thick black thighs
runs swiftly backwards then fast forward
unwinding self in a fierce sprint
knees chopping, hands sawing salt spray.

From dense clouds outbursts dazzling sun
stippling, dappling, spangling sea.
Young blonde lady rides roan mare
gently trots in calm curling tide
while fox terrier poops, prances away
with foxy look when I whistle to him.
Across beige beach cool breeze whips,
two tall young men approach, they're women
in windbreakers, slacks and short cropped hair.
Gulls patiently wait for apple core,
parliament of birds encircling blanket
peck and pounce when I heave it in air.

With faded jeans and bowie knife,
birdfeather in pocket, curly youth
stoops to forage pebbles on beach.
"You never know what you pick up," he says.
I nod and wonder: *double entendre?*
When time comes to change into pants
from nowhere people materialize
on horseback, foot, and helicopter:
out of the blue you're uncovered, stripped
bare when most free and innocent.
Dark clouds vanish, many more come,
variations on very October light.

San Francisco, 5.x.83

Friendship

Are we living
in the same city?
Are we empty-handed, empty-minded
sacks of wind and dust? Believe me,
he writes, I'm your friend, in spite
of my failure to appear, my "broken"
promises. I lack
stamina to face
things. I answer: Ah,
yes, one changes, grows
bored, drops a lover, a friend. No,
he writes, he hasn't the courage to come
around. Vows to cure himself

of breaking his word. Signs, As ever,
your Eternal Friend. Shows up
a year later. I
love you, he says sincerely, but
my fatigue is monumental. Can't
stay long, I have a dinner date. You
should grow your sideburns longer. I'll
come back in a week. A year passes.
Out of the blue he writes: If not
temporal, I'm your eternal friend.
Are we poets or what? Who are we?
Anyway, I miss you. I wish
I could see you, talk to you,
grow close again. I reply:
I feel much better now
that I've given up hope.

San Francisco, 6.v.84

Rescue Remedy

1

From now on I want each moment
of roses and Ravel like a surge
of sound and sea cloudburst of harps
catching a glimpse of feeling
   momentarily escaping
   into the psychic sense
that holds and binds us
   in music and touch

I saw you in the rainbow
shopping for organic flageolets
t-shirt and cutoffs revealing shots
of dazzling muscle as you bent over
   pleased to be living at this hour
   with so many of you laid out
   like a twelve-tone row
not a sewing machine or umbrella
   construct of need
   tingling my spine
      blinding erection

oh the felony of unbuttoned flies
assault and battery of good looks
  immorality of being alive
    orgasm of death crime of coming

2

I think these clouds are going to collide
with my thoughts. Will the Rescue Remedy
save me? the Star of Bethlehem? sweet
chestnut? the black pansy perhaps?
  will the mimulus help? for fear
  of known things such as heights
      or *other people?* will vervain
    protect me from those who have
strong opinions? and sweet chestnut
      from those who feel
they have reached the limit of their
      endurance? and
despite the larch that may guard me
from anticipating failure and refusing
to make a real effort to succeed
  I'm thrown into reverse
  by fear of gay massacre
and withering away
        before my time
    with a trendy disease.

3

Yes, poison is in. Everything
we eat drink see or fuck
    the air we breathe
    the sea we surf
even our cum gives birth to death.

  Brightnesse doth not fall from the Aire
  Queens must die young and faire
    Love, have Mercy on my Soul

All 38 remedies come in liquid concentrate form
  reputed to have a positive calming and
        stabilizing effect
in most stressful situations including

nervousness anxiety anguish desperation
just take a few drops of the Rescue Remedy
for everyday stresses such as
taking exams making speeches bad loans
job interviews

oak for those who struggle on despite despondencies
olive for mental and physical exhaustion
sapped vitality with no reserve
mustard for deep gloom
crab apple for those who feel something is not
quite clean about themselves
gorse for feelings of hopelessness and futility
holly for negative feelings
and a need for love

4

organic rice cakes! unsalted millet!
10 drops of chaparral! pau d'arco
from Argentina! hawthorn berries and green
Savoy cabbage leaves! will
this remedy work for bad luck?
bad dreams? will it heal
fanatic assassins on suicide missions?
godly nuts leveling
everything in sight
with hollow mechanical expressions?
will it free us to play
in sand and sun and swim
hot crotches together
with singing limbs?

ritual practices like
talking or praying to a plant
or making an offering before picking it
will raise one's consciousness

as we stroll on country paths
often a plant will greet us with a loud scent
shouting to us that the sense
of smell has a direct link with
the subconscious mind as Proust
has proven in six volumes
of memory and lust
such herbs can be used in dream pillows

for closer touch with our
emotional depths
aromatic herbs such as mugwort sandalwood pennyroyal
rose bay sage/make your peace with them
they will take care of you
herbs have feelings too
don't kill them take bits and pieces
and leave the rest
don't mug the mugwort
be sage
toxins must go

wood betony for self-loathing skullcap for feeling absurd
slippery elm for difficulty in believing in others or self
gota kola for schizophrenia lemon balm for paranoia
(finding ourselves in places and life situations
we can't accept)
smoke tussilago with cannabis for inflamed ego
cascara sagrada for anal retention chickweed for gluttony
calamus to quit smoking and calm the nerves
(also treats scabies lice and crabs)
fo-ti-tieng for premature aging ginseng for potency
fu ling for fearfulness and feelings of insecurity
buchu with uva ursi for the prostate gland
echinacea for v.d. and the immune system
burdock's an aphrodisiac
kava kava invokes deep sleep and full-length epic dreams
and goldenseal's good for everything.

San Francisco, 9.x.84

Medieval Spectre

The kid is cute (quite innocent)
but horrified at his deviate lust
he threw himself from a topfloor window
broke his back and grew a moustache.

A boyfriend deflowered him but
technically he remains a virgin
no penetration having taken place
in the years of the plague.

A medieval spectre haunts sex.

San Francisco, 1985

In the Cafes

(After Cavafy)

In the cafés, smoky and noisy,
and the loud bars with their screeching
and punk rock madness that deafens me
I'm bored. I've never cared for
these trashy joints. But they're good for drowning
persistent echoes of Keith. Quite suddenly
he left, without warning, for the proud
owner of two Porsches and a big house in Marin,
a hot tub and swimming pool. Keith, I don't doubt,
has tender feelings for me still. Yet I'm sure
he has learned to develop tender feelings
for a man with two Porsches. I live
in squalor. But what stays fresh
and sweet, what keeps me going, is
that for two whole months I had Keith,
the most desirable youth
on Polk Street. None
could compare with him. In my drab flat
with a view of trash cans and parking lots
he lived with me, a warm
affectionate lover—there was surely more to him
than meets the eye—mine not for a mansion
and two fast Porsches.

San Francisco, 29.ix.85

In a Cafe-Bar

(After Verlaine)

Remember the café-bar crowded with pricks
With their stupid morals and straight loves,—dumb hicks!
Where we alone, we two, bore the label "queer,"
But didn't give a shit and whacked it right there
Under their noses in fact (what a great joke
We played on them discreetly, veiled by the smoke
From our pipes: like Io fucking with Zeus)
Until our cocks, bursting with love-juice

From our manipulations, like a bomb
Under the table shot great jets of cum.

San Francisco, 1985

High School Lover

slant blue gaze
high cheekbones   pouting lips
in bathroom mirror admiring
his astonishing features
and first moustache
(pastel smudge on upper lip)
small upturned nose
and luminous wide eyes
that attract wherever he goes
longing looks for those
superb thighs and tell
tale bulge of pleasure

doing homework
nodding in rhythm to some hot
jamming earphones
thick hair standing up a little
framing forehead ears face
bent over geometry
perfect buttocks
partly exposed
he lies on the floor
white gym socks soiled   tennis shoes torn
from rough wear of power slides
on skateboard with fiery blue
dragon and skullsword emblem
surface smeared by the city

withal a cheerful cherub
streetwise tender tough
ray of sunshine breakdancing
nude and high in bedroom
with laughter and bad breath
(pot beer cigarettes)
mouth full of fun

and kisses
half-child half-man
balanced in wild abandon
of anarchy
and hotblooded joy

in search of never ending touch
at times of need selling
the firm young flesh
for immediate satisfaction
and dollars
to quell the hunger
in growing cells
he grows and gladdens the heart
of girls and fatherly
lone men

San Francisco, 2.x.85

Lost America

discs of lost america!   gray pearl saxophone
riffs of body & soul   & smoke gets in your eyes
stardust   blue heaven   as time goes by
musical comedy romance   of wanting to be
beautiful & great

the tenor sax digs deep in proustian key
unearthing mouldy sneakers   lockerrooms
pubic shadows   in chlorine pools
bare boythighs   and buttocks of
secret loves in fiery crackle   and static
of worn old platters   that patina of sound

sound & smell filtered thru   pubescence
waking fearful pleasure-petals
in the groin   discovered thrill
of come

sweet coffee smell   of dusky docks
i cover the waterfront   where are you?
old songs stuck in the memory   desires lingering
the east river crawls   across the page

Athens, 1965/*San Francisco,* 1985

Old Black Remington

Old black Remington noiseless, what shall we type today?
is there room among your keys? for real feelings? cool moods?
I stare out the window at Mutual Life; then examine my palm,
headline slopes down depressed but the fateline, ah, it's
still good, still strong, though at the wrist a chain of
snarled emotions tells the story, and the lifeline's still scary,
so much left unsaid undone, old poets dying, o river run,
Kerouac Patchen Pound, and yes they will stay fresh for ages
having pierced the dark with lasers of insight, cut through
black voids with shapely music, enlightened our doldrums,
lifted us, made us laugh and rage...oh, what about me,
mount of Apollo, am I immortal? hmmm, soon be worthless bone,
a book, a shade, a poem in secondhand bookstore, a bit dusty, sure;
some sexy youth will praise my name but I won't care, so here's
another poem, and thanks, old black Remington noiseless.

San Francisco, 1972/1985

Unknown Destination

1

Fifteen men are in love with him.
One is Ma Bell.
Another flies in from Switzerland,
heads a chemical firm.

"He just wants to see me smile.
I smile,
He gives me a Mercedes.
Flies back on the next plane
without touching me."

Fifteen men who run the world.
He runs them. They lick his toes.

2

In the house of glass you can see through
to the floor below. And the floor below
the floor below. All glass. You can see
down to the silver and gold plumbing.

On the walls are plates of gold.
You can't see through them.
The banker offers his house and his bank.
With devastating charm the boy barely
acknowledges them. It is his due.

Industrialists, tycoons, politicians—he
pisses on them. This inspires reverence.
They fall to their knees, content with a taste,
a smell, a close view of his "parts." They whimper
and lose consciousness.

3

Here is his leather pouch.
Bulging with green.
He will spend it tonight.
He will spend it on a party.
MDA. Quaaludes. Cocaine.
Brownies. Columbian. Boys.

Fifteen world leaders
are mad for him.
His nineteenth birthday party
will be an international event.

4

"The man I love must love only me.

I'll put a chastity belt on him.
Once a year I'll unlock the belt. Make love
for one night. He must wait all year
for this. Must not see anyone.
Must not jack off. Just pee
through the hole.

I'll make him rich. Seven thousand a month.
Just to wait for me. If he breaks out of that belt
and fucks anyone else
                                    I'll scalp him.
I'll tear off his nose. Rip out his jaw.
Half a face. That's what I'll leave.
I have a fourth in Tai Kwan-do.
Learned it in Korea.

Listen.
A trick last week—
after we partied I fell asleep.
My house boy wakes me. 'He's
got your billfold,' he says.

I go to the living room. In the darkness I see him
by the window. I switch on the light. He's removing the
green. 'I wouldn't do that,' I say. He grins. 'What
are ya gonna do about it?' 'I don't like that,' I say. He grins.
I rip off his nose. I hand it to him.

He stands there with his nose in his hand.
Screaming.

'Call an ambulance!' he screams.

'Get out or I'll rip off your jaw!' I say.

He runs out, bleeding all over my Persian rug.

I woulda gave him the green if he'd of asked.

He was beautiful. Flawless. His face *was* flawless.

I'm looking for just one man
who really loves me."

5

His striped t-shirt is in tatters.
Tight white cords smudged and stained.

He hangs around the café till closing time.

He will buy the café, he says. Hire
the most beautiful boys.
Wants us to know he is powerful.
The most powerful force on the planet.
He pulls the strings behind the leaders.
Governments wait for his orders.

Soon he must leave on his private plane
for an unknown destination.

San Francisco, 1.ii.82/85

From **Watcher in the Sky**

Sebastian Rainbow had no choice. He spreadeagled
In the iconic position. Times were getting hard
For crucifixion addicts. The guy nearly tore him open
With his belaying pin. In the straw hut at the edge
Of town. But to Sebastian, who was used
To far greater pain and humiliation
It served merely as another trial to be patiently endured
On his way to the Watcher in the Sky.
On the bamboo wall hung a single picture
Whose eyes penetrated Rainbow's. No matter which way he turned
The eyes followed. He lay with a straw-filled pillow
Under his midriff, looking up at the eyes and thorns, admiringly.
Blood gushed from an open heart that seemed to palpitate and throb
With every bang of the dong. Mesmerized by tongues
Of flame in the man's eyes, black pupils like nails hammered into his brain,
The man's immensity filled the skies. Blue clouds hovered
Around long silky hair. White space spread
Like ocean waves. Infinite foam of space. He felt
Seized with immeasurable awe. It was Easter.

*

Every Good Friday scores of young men pour into the city
Using real nails on real crosses, shoving and fighting
And kicking each other to get their chance to be hung
Symbolized, perhaps, by chrome-plated jeepney taxis
That look like rolling pinball machines; this gangster economy
Provides everything from call-girls to crucifixions.
Scores of poets volunteer for actual crucifixion
In a free-wheeling economy that actually ignores them.
Our founding fathers considered these volunteer Christs
A national treasure. Each will be accompanied by a certificate
Guaranteeing his authenticity—plus an account
Of the crucifixion, in detail. Even those
Poets who were never involved
Long ago attracted to themselves a romantic connection,
Spanish and English buccaneers or French accursed seers—
Corbière, Rimbaud, Laforgue, and of course Isidore Ducasse,
Who burned the stale props of the 19th-century charnel houses
And when their ignored works were discovered after early deaths
Became the role models for successful crucifixion.
This pattern has held for over a century

And still persists, so prepare yourself again
For a genuine red-blooded American crucifixion
As Baudelairean buccaneers earn another questionable triumph
Of self-denial over temporal indifference.

*

Yellow heavens, trunk of stars,
    tin angels with leather wings
and pasteboard clouds,
                    medallions
    of Bleeding Hearts,

hoarse cries of boys
    in summer heat
        slant room
  musty with smells, old
underwear, moldy photos,
    report cards

(goldenrod and couchgrass
              in vacant lots
    and washing flurries
        by cracked brick walls)

Dardanella
    through raspy lily-horn
trailing stale whiffs of
        flaky newsprint,
           sweetness of lavender

sachets,
stiff rubber bands,
        tang
    of old face powder,
motheaten handerchiefs—

address unknown,
    forgotten,
        vanished
with close relations

into that morgue of treasures,
    catcalls,

                    wisps of voices
                        fading
                            whispering
            withering faces—

leaning
        from attic window
        over the ironbarred bank
            beneath the gables
                stuffy with rot
                    and sweat

hearing
            parents grunting
                battling
            under the sticky eaves
in the summer night

in the trap
        of time
        in a small
                    space

asking
        What
                lies beyond?
        Who
                am I now?
sailing out the window
        into a circle of light

entering
        a secret newsreel
                of real life

seeing
        human tides
                    flowing
swirling
        forms, faces, limbs,

my singular wave
        merged in the human tide

a Vision!
    a universe!

Then vastness shrank
       shriveled
  in a heart benumbed
    with Time
though held in memory, a
   Mystery, a
       Poem.

San Francisco, 1984/85

VI. HOMO
(1984-1985)

Homo

Amber lamplight on the
Green canal. Leaves falling
Into the ripples. Gulls
Settle on bridges. In Amsterdam
I lean from the attic window
Under the eaves in this
16th Century brick house, the
Trap door pulls up and
Conceals the bedroom, an Anne Frank
Dutch device that saved the
Lives of many Jews. The
Bedroom also contains
A meditation room with
Fine Persian carpets and glass
Roof, forming a triangle.
Beside me on the futon lies
The young student who followed me
After my readings and seminar
At the university. We
Made love all night. He is tall
With enormous gray luminous eyes.
Next day at the Van Gogh museum
Before the drawings of old peasants
In the Brabant he touches the glass
Frames: "This could be my grandmother. See
This old man—my grandfather!" He was born
There, his family still lives there. He
Explains that nothing has changed
Since Vincent depicted them. His
Grandparents still bend and
Dig up turf and potatoes, the
Faces in the drawings are
Suddenly alive, close, real.
Germans on the border in Holland,
Dutch for hundreds of years. He
Is the only one to attend a
University—vivid applecheeked
Skin glows, large eyes shine
With the flame of Rimbaud and Van Gogh.

We lean over original letters from Vincent
To Theo under the glass case and he reads

Them and translates for me as we attract
Mild stares of curiosity by our clearly
Intimate pleasure in each other and our love
For this moment together—older man
With gray temples, short and dark,
Extremely tall youth with shock
Of honey hair, enjoying each other immensely.

Richard, I want to fix you in this poem
As firmly as Van Gogh fixed your ancestors
In his immortal sketches. I pray for this.

On the border, speaking Flemish, Dutch and German,
The people in the drawings like those of Brueghel or Bosch
Before them are closed, thick-featured, earthen, suspicious,
The bodies heavy-limbed. They've never changed. We lean over
The letters and he reads them aloud in a
Resonant deep voice and translates them for me.

*

Teeming with youth these northern cities
Of Europe stir the nesting urge
Though not for the opposite
Gender, as one might suppose. Fresh-
Faced and enticingly well-
Made, with voluptuous
Lips and ruddy pale complexions,
Eyes the color of sky,
Young males with deep
Voices and applecheeked schoolboy
Ways have the flirtatious air and
Smooth skin of babes. But
Nothing girlish, believe me, or
Babyish about their hard
Bodies and often prominent
Protuberance between
Agile legs; the magic
Wand keeps them saucy, they
Sing in the streets of Zurich or
Amsterdam eager as kids
With darting eyes. Their trousers cling
Skintight to knifesharp thighs. Nothing
Can stem the longed-for same-sex need,

No matter what man-made laws may cause
In suffering. Wherever you go
The tide of sexuality swells
For same-sex love. With few exceptions
Most countries shut hearts and minds
Against it, slam a dike or dam
On nature. Well, this may work with water
But not the sexual tide. In
The Philippines blackmail attends
Each act of "affection," and
Extortion and deportation greet
The unwary tourist. Rackets
Flourish where unjust laws prevail.
Once the land of free and easy
Love between males, now it's a trap.
In the Moslem world where the Rubaiyat
And Sufi poems extolled boy-love
The fundamentalist police
Chop noses, hands, feet, necks and dicks
Off for this universal need.
In the Soviet Union and its iron bloc
Torture, exile and slavery
Greet "decadent bourgeois acts"
Like tenderness of men
For men, women for women, as if
Sex could be legislated and made
Politically correct. No head
Is screwed on straight. *Chez nous*
In the USA Gay men and boys
Are bashed and killed with impunity
In the name of *God,* no less. The world
Has gone berserk with politics
And sick, depraved religion. Murder,
Their lingua franca, prevails. Nuts
Quote the Bible and Koran
Convincing us we're better off dead
And try to prove it as fast as they can.
In Rumania if you're caught with your pants
Down in *flagrante* you can tell the police
That your Rumanian comrade was buying them.
The young men will peel for American jeans.

*

We live under dictatorship
Whether of God or man.
Stalin is said to have deported
All Russian homosexuals
To the Arctic Circle, Tschaikowsky
Murdered by the Czar
For an affair with a young
Prince. The imperial doctor injected him
With typhus—to avoid a scandal.
Swan Lake and *Sleeping Beauty*
Could not save him. *Eugene Onegin*
And *Pique Dame* could not save a sacred
Hair of his beard. The Czar wept.
No other course presented itself.
(The Empire must be maintained.)
Russia's greatest composer martyred
For homosexuality.
Gogol, "Mother of the Russian Novel,"
Also involved with a prince, died
Young, thus avoiding homocide.

    How many homosexuals
    Would Rexroth have exiled to Siberia?
    How many Jews would Pound
    Have gassed at Auschwitz and Buchenwald?
    How many Otto René Castillos
    Can Guatemala burn at the stake?
    How many Roque Daltons
    Can El Salvador liquidate?
    How many major poets
    Can condone mass murder and torture?
    How long can civilization
    Stamp its boot on the human face?

*

Living below the poverty line
Having dedicated my life
To the Muse I travel
From San Francisco to Amsterdam,
Zurich and back (paid all ways
To read my poems, put up in hotels,
Third-class, grungy, cheap) and earn
Less than the cost of plane-fare—strange
Profession, or calling, rather,

Rewarded mostly by shy smiles, a
Schoolboy now and then with misty
Eyes and hero-worship who
Follows us to a café, writes
His name, address: "If you return...
Perhaps we'll meet again?..." He
Hopes you'll answer his letters. Will
Some dream come true, change
Your life and his? This
Happened to Auden and Verlaine.
In the wings waits some raw Rimbaud,
Some talented, arrogant youth who'll
Turn your life inside out with
Ecstasy and suffering. Yes,
Auden's Rimbaud did that
To him and me. After two years
He cruelly refused to bed with Auden
Who turned homicidal with rage
And jealousy: "I was forced to know
What it's like to feel oneself the prey
Of demonic powers, in both the Greek
And Christian sense, stripped
Of self-control and self-respect,
Behaving like a ham-actor in
A Strindberg play." How
Can biographers know the facts
Third-hand of what we felt
And did, and what we said or who
Loved, envied, undermined, betrayed
Whom? Who was the villain, who
The victim? The Superstar
Can do no wrong, the lesser shines
More dimly, fades, and sputters out
Into a black hole as time forgives
The one whose words still blaze with light
Into a future century
His life and deeds remote from truth.

*

"Mad, bad and dangerous to know,"
Wrote Lady Caroline Lamb in her diary
The night she first met Lord Byron. He
Had no use for prudes and said so—
He refused to compromise

With social reticence on sex.
(In Venice when Shelley asked
Why he was always surrounded by rough
Young men Byron replied: "What I earn
With my brains I spend on my arse." Shelley
Left.) Byron's memoirs were
Destroyed by his English publisher.
Too outrageous. Too obscene.
His journals and letters reveal that he
Had incestuous fun with his half-sister
And describe a party they both attended:
"Countesses and ladies of fashion left
The room in droves," he wrote. But many
More threw themselves at his feet—wives
And daughters of the nobility,
Governesses and servant girls.
He threw himself at the feet
Of gondoliers and stable-boys.
Today only rock and film stars compare
With his effect on the public. Shelley
Wrote: "An exceedingly interesting person
But a slave to the vilest and most vulgar
Prejudices, and mad as the winds."
By which, presumably, he meant
His undisguised love of working-class boys.
Shelley, alas, was a frightful prude
For all his anarchistic faith.
(And probably a closet-case, too.)
Byron in every act and breath
Was a flaming iconoclast to the bone,
Revolutionary for human rights
Centuries ahead of his time.
Of poor Keats he wrote rather callously:
"A Bedlam vision produced by raw pork
And opium." Matthew Arnold wrote
Of all three: "Their names will be greater than
Their writings." Their memory lingers on.
Byron practised what he preached:
"Ordered promiscuity."
He found it most in Italy
The most sensual and sensible
Of Western nations, the country of love
In all its forms, and the country of beauty.
Oppose this to England, the country of duty
And you will understand Byron completely.

In the Coliseum he once invoked
Nemesis to curse his wife's
Lawyer—with great success, it seems,
For later the man cut his own throat.
What all the biographies skirt
When they describe his exploits we
Can now fill in: when they write of his women
"With great black eyes and fine figures—fit
To breed gladiators from" they don't
Tell us how much he enjoyed their sons,
The gladiators he went down on.

*

Ever since Justinian
Who wanted more power over the Church
Fifteen-hundred years ago
Passed the first law against same-sex love
With the perfectly logical excuse
That homosexuality
Caused earthquakes, we have seen
Religion and politics
Condemn gay sex as crime and sin.
The law had no effect upon
The population; they behaved
As if the Emperor had gone mad.
But some prominent bishops lost
Their bishoprics and balls,
Were tortured and exiled. Many more
Churchmen were castrated and died.
The best historian of the time,
Procopius, states these harsh laws
Served as a pretext against the Greens
(The Emperor's circus opposition)
Or those "possessed of great wealth or
Who happened to have done something
Which offended the rulers." We know the empress
Theodora used the laws against
Personal enemies. When a young Green
Made some nasty remark about her
She charged him with homosexuality,
Had him castrated without trial.
Procopius says that this cruel law
Was invented chiefly to extort money
From the victims among whom were numbered

Pagans, unorthodox Christians, astrologers.
All Constantinople turned against
Theodora and Justinian
On this matter, as did other
Imperial cities. The Church itself
Was a prime target of the civil law
And played no part in its enactment.

Later the Church got into the act.
The Spanish Inquisition threw
Faggots into the fire to burn
Witches and other heretics,
Especially the uncoverted Jew.
Thus for a mad millennium
Or two the world has been in the grip
Of the criminally insane:
Neros, Caligulas, Justinians,
Torquemadas, Savonarolas,
Stalins, Hitlers, Mussolinis,
Cromwells, Falwells and Khomeinis.

*

Turning the last page of the calendar
I read the quotation for
December 1984: "If
You want a picture of the future,
Imagine a boot stamping on
A human face forever." Orwell.
I've lived to see it. From
The Spanish Civil War to this
Month, witnessing on a global
Scale the march of crime, a
Technicolor horror worse
Than the sterile murders on
Your TV screen (cosmetic).

> *Antisemitism is*
> *An exceptional folly*
> *In the roster of lunacy*

Wrote Kenneth Rexroth. On the very
Next page he commits "an exceptional
Folly" with homophobic rot.
Having criticized Pound's antisemitism

Rexroth erupts with equally gross
Hatred of "American Fairies."
"Homosexuality
is the revolt of the timid," he writes
With the same penetrating
Insight Pound showed for the "yids."
Rexroth has his "fairies" to kick
Around but admires the Jews. Well, what's
So timid about the Army of Lovers
Or Alexander the Great? What
About the drag queens who fought the police
On Christopher Street? What about
Julius Caesar? Lawrence of Arabia?

    Homophobia is
    An exceptional sickness
    In psychopathology
    Akin to antisemitism
    And Negrophobia

*

Collaged bits of reality
From various points on the planet.
Testimonials to shame. Our poets
Contribute to oppression.
Ridicule the innocent. Our
"Enlightened" poets goosestep
With swastika or hammer and sickle,
Condescending and patronizing
While praising universal love.
Love in the abstract. On
Individual humans they spit.
Abuse and torture of the innocent
By verbal vivisection
Is cruel and wanton as
Laboratory experiments
On helpless animals
By well-meaning but dense doctors
Believing beasts don't suffer. Does
It ever occur to them they may be
Wrong? Ego blinds them. They're
Gods and demigods. Poets
And doctors dispense their pills

And nostrums for the good of the race
Often making matters worse.

Remember the drag queens in Greenwich Village
Who fought the cops with their fists and any
Available objects? They
Sparked Gay Liberation, an
Unprecedented event
Equivalent to the Warsaw Ghetto
Uprising of the Jews against
Vastly superior Nazi might.
Once ignited the spirit
Does not die. Israel rose
From the ashes of the Warsaw Ghetto,
Gay Rights rose from the ghetto
On Christopher Street. It
Is better to die fighting than
To live on your knees. Krishna was right
To admonish Arjuna when he refused
To fight his kin to the death. His brothers
Would have finished him off.
Pacifism does not work. I say this
Sadly. We're up against
Ignorant armies and must
Defeat them or die.

*

Love is not a crime;
If it were a crime to love
God would not have bound
Even the divine with love.

(Carmina Burana)

*

The Greek and Roman poets were Gay:
Virgil, Ovid, Horace, Catullus,
Martial, Juvenal, Tibullus.
Where would our culture be without them?
(Gay-basher Rexroth, Jew-baiter Pound
Through verbal abuse contributed
To genocide and fagocide—

Much is the Moral Majority
Sees God's punishment on the victims
Of AIDS, blaming the patient for
The disease. Who'll cure the Moral
Morons of terminal stupidity?)
Euripides at seventy-two
Spoke of his love for Agathon
Who was forty: "A fine Autumn
Is a beautiful thing indeed!"
Anacreon, who "delighted in
Young men" confided, "I'm old,
There's no denying it. So what?
Among young satyrs I can dance as well
As old Bacchus himself!" When asked
Why his poems were always about young boys
And not about gods he replied: "That
Is because young boys *are* our gods."
He was a pleasure-loving, wine-loving
Boy-loving poet. "Whatever Plato
May say it is unlikely that
Handsome Alciabiades,
After sleeping beneath the same blanket
As Socrates, arose intact
From his embraces," Lucian wrote.
Dying at eighty in the gymnasium,
His head on the knees of a boy, Pindar
Seemed happily asleep
When the attendant came to wake him.
Sophocles at fifty-five
Confessed that despite his age
He often fell in love with boys.
And Aristophanes wrote
That the favorite occupation
Of sophists and intellectuals
Was to make the rounds of gymnasiums
To pick up boys.
They went to their lessons
Accompanied by their little friends.
At twelve a boy already
Appealed to them, says the great playwright.
They considered him in the prime of life
Between sixteen and seventeen.
At eighteen he was over the hill.

*

To have a father of some handsome lad
Come up and chide me with complaints like these:
Fine things I hear of you, Stilbonides,
You met my son returning from the baths,
And never kissed, or hugged, or fondled him,
You, his paternal friend! You're a nice fellow!

(*The Birds,* Aristophanes)

*

And Addeus of Macedonia
(ca. 323 B.C.):

When you meet a lad who catches your fancy, do not waste any time
trying to disguise your intentions, but immediately grab hold of his
balls with both your hands. Do not mince words, or say, 'I respect
you' or 'I would like to be like a brother to you,' for that sort of thing
will only stand in your way.

*

Men are not gods
what you think
is somebody's
tall shadow over
your mind and
sometimes it looks
like a cross

*

Thought comes from the Devil?
    Good...to die?   "Thought
crimes" police
read one Book, distortions
        (5000 years of it)   brook
no argument.   Each word   beyond
Reason.   Beyond Thought.
    makes me puke.   hold views
of street-corner thugs   dumb hicks.
    Xianity for bucks. TV
evangelists screw   the simple-minded.

*

Zurich/Amsterdam, November, 1984/*San Francisco,* October, 1985

Grateful acknowledgments to the following publications in which some of these poems first appeared: *The London Magazine, Poetry Now, Gay Sunshine, Kayak, The Outsider, City Lights Journal, Beatitude, El Corno Emplumado, Invisible City, Gay Liberation Book, Suck, Olé, The Beat Diary, Entrails, Montana Gothic, Cosmos, Isis, Transatlantic Review, Laugh Literary, Between Worlds, La Bas, Klactoveedsedsteen, Residu, Unmuzzled Ox, Strange Faeces, City Magazine of San Francisco, Mirage, Soup, Osiris, Christopher Street, Nambla Journal, The Ark, Poetry Flash.* My apologies to any magazine I may have forgotten about. They have also appeared in the following anthologies: *The Male Muse, Angels of the Lyre, 185, Penguin Modern Poets 13, Practicing Angels,* and *The Penguin Book of Homosexual Verse.* Special thanks to City Lights Publishing Co. for permission to reprint from my book *Hotel Nirvana,* San Francisco 1974, the following poems: "I'm Not a Man," "We Bumped Off Your Friend the Poet," "I Am in the Hub of the Fiery Force," "Island of Giglio," "To Mohammed at the Café Central," "To Mohammed on Our Journeys," "To Mohammed in the Hotel of the Palms," and "I Would Not Recommend Love." Thanks to Nothing Doing in London 1966 and Panjandrum Press in San Francisco 1974 for permission to reprint "Karma Circuit" from my book *Karma Circuit*; and to the Macmillan Co. for permission to reprint "The Search" and "Victor Emmanuel Monument" from my book *The Dancing Beasts.* "I Am Going to Fly through Glass" and "Naked Men in Green Heated Water" (under the title "Only the Music Is Not Silent") originally appeared in my chapbook *I See America Daily,* published by Mother's Hen, San Francisco, 1974; and for the three Belli translations thanks to Jargon Society, Highlands, N. Carolina (1960), and Perivale Press, Van Nuys (1974). Acknowledgments for some of the manuscripts from the Norse Archive to the Lilly Library, Indiana University at Bloomington.

Thanks to Neeli Cherkovski for his moral support and suggestions, Robert Gluck for valuable advice, Floyd Conaway and Kevin Killian for their generous assistance and Dr. William R. Horstman, Robert Goldstein, and Kennith Moore for being there.